# SCENERY
## BY THE
# SEASONS

Edited by Randy Rehberg

KALMBACH BOOKS

**Kalmbach Books**
21027 Crossroads Circle
Waukesha, Wisconsin 53186
www.Kalmbach.com/Books

Published in 2010
14 13 12 11 10   1 2 3 4 5

Manufactured in the United States of America
ISBN: 978-0-89024-717-4

"Trees from garden plants," "Lily pads, cattails, and pond scum," "Easy autumn trees," and some material from "Corn on the strip and other crops" appeared previously in *Model Railroader* magazine. "Winter along the Timber Trail" appeared previously in *Classic Toy Trains* magazine.

Cover photos: Front (clockwise from top)—David Popp, Mike Danneman, Cody Grivno
Back (from top)—David Popp, Lance Mindheim, Paul Dolkos, Mike Danneman

## About the authors

**Mike Confalone** is publisher of *Railroad Explorer* magazine. He has been modeling since he was 11 years old. Mike lives in Goffstown, N.H., with his wife, Susan, and son, Thomas.

**Mike Danneman** is a professional illustrator as well as a contributor to *Model Railroader* magazine. Mike lives in Arvada, Colo., and is well known for his N scale Denver & Rio Grande layouts.

**Paul Dolkos** is a veteran model railroader and a frequent contributor to *Model Railroader* and *Model Railroad Planning*. He lives in Virginia and recently began a new layout based on Baltimore's harbor district.

**Cody Grivno** is an associate editor for *Model Railroader* magazine. Trains have been a part of his life from an early age. Cody is an avid railfan and also enjoys painting and detailing freight cars and locomotives.

**Kent Johnson** is an associate editor for *Model Railroader* magazine and senior editor for *Classic Toy Trains*. Kent and his wife, Ella, are the parents of two sons. His layout is inspired by his travels to western Canada.

**Gerry Leone** is a master model railroader. His Bona Vista Railroad was featured in *Great Model Railroads 2008*. It is a freelanced road set in the Midwest in 1953. Gerry lives in Minnesota with his wife, Renay.

**Horst Meier** is a contributor to *Model Railroader*. He lives in Frankfort, Germany, and has written several books on model railroading. Horst models an HO scale Union Pacific layout.

**Lance Mindheim** owns a custom layout-building company. He and his wife, Cathy, have a son, Zachary, who accompanies Lance to model railroad events. Lance enjoys rooting for the Washington Redskins.

**David Popp** is managing editor for *Model Railroader* magazine. David enjoys slot car racing, gardening, and video production. He lives in Waterford, Wis., with his wife, Ingrid, and her grand piano.

**Publisher's Cataloging-In-Publication Data**

Scenery by the seasons / edited by Randy Rehberg.

   p. : col. ill. ;  cm. -- (Model railroader books. Model railroader's how-to guide)

   Some material has previously appeared in Model railroader magazine and Classic toy trains magazine.

   ISBN: 978-0-89024-717-4

1. Railroads--Models.  2. Railroads--Models--Design and construction--Handbooks, manuals, etc.  I. Rehberg, Randy.
II. Title: Model railroader.  III. Title: Classic toy trains.

TF197 .S24 2010

625.1/9

# Contents

by David Popp

This spring scene on Mike Danneman's layout is just one example of what you can do to model scenes with nature at its finest. *Photo by Mike Danneman*

Spring is a time of sharp contrasts to most other seasons. It begins with the muted, dull colors of winter. In early spring, piles of dirty, crusty snow stubbornly hang on in the shadowed areas of the landscape. Until the frost is completely out of the ground, the top layer of earth becomes saturated with water, turning it into a sea of squishy mud. However, as the days lengthen, winter eventually releases its grip, and life begins to seep out of the gloom. (It just takes longer in New England; see Chapter Three.)

Overnight, with the first warm weather and a good thunderstorm, it seems as though nature has opened a paint store. First, the grass becomes surprisingly green. Then, by mid-spring, the landscape is filled with the colors of early blooming plants, such as pink and white cherry blossoms, yellow daffodils, and tulips in lush reds, bright pinks, and other hues. Next, the trees bud out, and their new leaves unfold in bright greens that sometimes look almost yellow.

By late May, the landscape can seem luminescent with life. At my home in southeastern Wisconsin, our dogwood hedge comes into full bloom just after Memorial Day, and the bushes are covered with white blossoms. At the same time, the dozens of lilac bushes in the yard burst forth with huge clusters of delicate purple flowers, so for a couple of weeks, a trip outside provides a visual treat.

For all its amazing color and promise of new life, spring is probably the season I've seen modeled least on layouts. Should you decide, however, that you wish to create a spring landscape for your model railroad, there are many products available to help you along the way. Various manufacturers offer flowering trees decorated in spring colors. Busch makes a variety of HO scale flowers, and a number of manufacturers offer brightly colored ground foam, so you can make your own flowering trees and shrubs.

Another important modeling feature for any spring scene is water. With the runoff from melted snow and the spring rains, rivers, streams, and creeks fill to overflowing during this season, which is a great opportunity for modeling waterfalls and rapids (Chapter Four). And spring is usually the one season where the dry creekbeds in arid regions of the country are filled with water. Convincing water scenery is fairly easy to make, and it never fails to impress and captivate visitors to your layout.

Finally, when modeling spring, don't forget the human element. If your layout is set in an agricultural area, you can model farmers at work planting crops in freshly plowed fields. In a more urban setting, you can model people doing spring-cleaning chores such as washing windows, hanging out rugs and linens to air out, sprucing up yards and gardens, and cleaning garages and automobiles—maybe even removing the snow tires.

With all of these great features and possibilities, spring offers a bounty of unique modeling opportunities.

1-1

CHAPTER ONE    by Mike Danneman

# Materials and colors

Choosing the right colors is a large part of correctly representing springtime in your scenery. In many parts of the country, the apparent color and texture difference between summer and spring greens might be subtle, but selecting the right colors will help you set the season, **1-1**.

**Three Krauss-Maffei diesel-hydraulic locomotives power a Rio Grande freight on my Moffat Road N scale layout. The spring-green grasses indicate the season I modeled. By summer, the grasses in this area are normally very yellow and brown due to the limited moisture found in this usually dry climate.**

**1-2**

Twelve-thousand horsepower worth of Tunnel Motors tug away at a westbound coal train near Tunnel 1. The surrounding hillsides are covered with the fresh colors of spring. I enhanced the Woodland Scenics ground foam with bright spring ground textures from Highball and AMSI.

**1-3**

The west local hits daylight as it emerges from the dark confines of Tunnel 2. Above the train, steep ledges show signs of spring as grasses begin to emerge from the rocky soils.

**1-4**

Sailing through a sea of green trees, this Burlington Northern intermodal train is eastbound on a beautiful Memorial Day weekend in 1993 at Cassville, Wis. Even though at first glance, all of the trees look the same color, you can see that there are subtle differences in the color tones in the expanse of trees.

Greens found in spring grasses and trees tend to be lighter and brighter than their summer equivalents. Most manufacturers of ground foam and other foliage materials have a good selection of summer colors. Since the spring season isn't modeled as often, these colors are not as common. If a particular brand you are using doesn't have spring colors, don't be afraid to cross over the aisle at the hobby shop to look at another brand.

My N scale Rio Grande Moffat Road layout is set in the springtime of the year. When purchasing spring-green colors of ground foam for the open expanses of the Big Ten Curve region of my layout, it took a few tries to get the grassy areas to look correct. At first, all the colors I tried were too dark, or summer-like. Then I found some products from Highball and AMSI that were lighter in tone and more spring-like in color that nicely lightened up the grassy areas on my scene, **1-2**.

In some areas of my layout, the rocky mountain scenery does not contain a lot of foliage. But even in these areas, such as the Front Range formation known as the Flatirons, the small amount of grasses that does grow among the rocks is green from recent spring snow and rain, **1-3**.

The same spring color principle applies to many deciduous trees. In springtime, the new growth is lighter and brighter green in color, **1-4**. Keep this in mind when purchasing or making trees for a spring setting. Another factor is how trees look in very early spring when only a few young leaves are emerging. Without a detailed and lacy armature to represent the tree's branches, this look is harder to accomplish. You'll need tree kits that include a well-detailed armature if you model trees with little foliage.

CHAPTER TWO    by David Popp

# Trees from garden plants

Most model railroads need an assortment of trees. Although there are many commercially available tree models on the market, sometimes it's more fun (and economical) to make your own. Years ago, my brother Christopher, who builds architectural models, taught me a technique he uses for making tree armatures from a common garden plant called sedum. I've since made a few refinements to the process, which results in great-looking foreground model trees for late spring and summer layouts, **2-1**.

**You can make great detailed foreground trees using a natural material from a plant called sedum.**

7

2-2

These common sedum plants have not yet flowered. After a few seasons, you can divide sedum to produce more plants, which will produce more trees for your layout.

2-3

Different varieties of sedum have differing sizes of flower heads and produce a mix of tree types.

2-4

Make the sedum stalks usable by soaking them in a diluted solution of matte medium.

2-5

Poke holes in a foam block to easily insert the drying stalks and set the block over a bucket to catch the drips.

2-6

The height of your trees will vary depending upon the scale you model. For N scale, use single pieces from 1½" to 3" tall. For HO scale trees, you can use pieces to 5" or taller.

2-7

When combining stalks, find stalks that fit together well and glue them together using cyanoacrylate adhesive (CA).

What is sedum? It's a hardy decorative perennial that grows in most regions of the United States, **2-2**. There are a number of varieties of this plant, but most produce varying heights and sizes of stalks with dense heads made up of many small pale pink or purple flowers. Sedum blooms in late summer and through most of the fall until the first hard freeze.

Admittedly, the very first part of this process, waiting for the sedum to grow, takes a bit longer than most other projects. And, once the sedum has grown, you also have to let it dry for several months before you can use it to make trees. One season's worth of sedum from just three or four healthy plants will make a lot of great-looking trees for your layout. However, if you don't have the time, space, or inclination to grow your own sedum, scope out your neighborhood for gardens that have the plants. Unless they're fellow modelers, most gardeners will let you have their sedum stalks in the fall, after the plants have finished blooming.

## Preparing the sedum

Sedum comes in several varieties, and I have plants that produce large and small flower heads, **2-3**. Before you can use the sedum, it must be dried. I typically leave the sedum stalks on the plants in the garden until late fall or early winter. I'll then clip them and leave them in a bushel basket in the garage to finish the drying process.

Dried sedum is brittle, so you need to treat it before you can make trees out of it. To treat the cuttings, fill a plastic container with one part matte medium and four parts water. After mixing the water and matte medium thoroughly, dip the sedum stalks into the liquid one stalk at a time, **2-4**. Give the sedum 15-20 seconds to soak up the matte medium. Then set the sedum aside to dry.

The stalks will dry straighter if you hang them upside down. I use a block of 2" foam insulation board to hold the sedum and then set the block upside down over a 5-gallon bucket, **2-5**. This protects the delicate flower heads and helps the stalks dry straight.

Once treated, the sedum will be more resilient and somewhat flexible, making it easier to use the material without damaging it.

## Building trees

Small trees, such as fruit trees or saplings, are the simplest types of trees to make of sedum because they use a single stalk. Select stalks that are straight and have a fairly even flower head. Trim the stalk to the preferred height using a sharp flush cutter for this step, **2-6**.

At this point, trim any flower heads and branches that may be broken or simply not to your liking. As always, use the trees you see in nature as a guide. Small trees can be fairly uneven, but mid-sized trees should have a full, rounded shape.

You can make bigger, fuller trees by combining two or more stalks of sedum, **2-7**. Hold or clamp the ends and then spread a medium-thickness cyanoacrylate adhesive (CA) between the trunks. Next, apply a drop or two of CA accelerator to speed up the adhesive's setting

2-8

When the caulk dries, use a hobby knife to carve away any parts of the caulk that don't look tree-like.

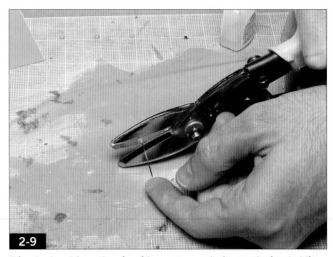

2-9

Trim the head from the pin with a cutter made for steel wire, holding the pinhead down and away from you.

2-10

Dip the modified pin in CA and insert it into the trunk.

2-11

Paint the trunks gray, not brown, as most tree bark is a gray color.

time. Once the CA has set, trim the trunk to the desired length.

More mature trees, such as old oaks, will require thicker trunks. After combining several stalks of sedum to form a larger tree, apply a layer of latex caulk to the trunk to thicken it, **2-8**. Work the caulk around the trunk and form a small flare at the base of the tree.

## Adding mounting pins

The trees will need mounting pins when they are inserted into a foam scenery base. I modified straight pins for this step. Trim the head from the pin using a cutter made for steel wire, **2-9**. Also, wear safety goggles and hold the pinhead down and away from you when making the cut.

The sedum stalks are hollow, making it fairly easy to install the pins. I start by inserting a regular straight pin into the base about a ¼" to open the hole. Next, I dip the cut end of a modified pin into a drop of CA and insert the pin into the hole, **2-10**. The pins not only make installing the trees on the layout much easier, but they also give you a convenient handle with which to hold the model trees while you're working on them.

## Painting the armatures

Before you can cover the tree with foliage, you need to paint it. Although you can airbrush the trees with most any acrylic paint, I like to work quickly, so I use a spray can of Rust-Oleum dark gray Automobile Primer, **2-11**. The important thing here is that you use a flat-finish paint, so your tree trunks aren't glossy. If you want to make birch

or aspen trees, use an off-white spray paint instead. You can add the black markings with a small paintbrush or marker later.

To spray the trees, I mount them to a cardboard box. I don't use foam blocks for this step because the organic solvent-based spray paint will dissolve the foam. Be sure to also spray the underside of the seed heads for even coverage.

## Finally, the leaves

Once the paint has dried, it's finally time to add the leaves. I use various types and colors of ground foam to simulate the leaves on the trees. This is where you'll need to do some shopping, as the grading of ground foam scenery materials varies between manufacturers. For these trees, I used Scenic Express EX805B Grass Green Fine, which in my estimation (particularly

# Other trees

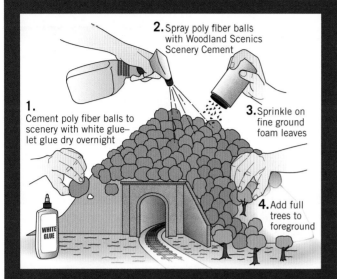

**1.** Cement poly fiber balls to scenery with white glue– let glue dry overnight

**2.** Spray poly fiber balls with Woodland Scenics Scenery Cement

**3.** Sprinkle on fine ground foam leaves

**4.** Add full trees to foreground

WHITE GLUE

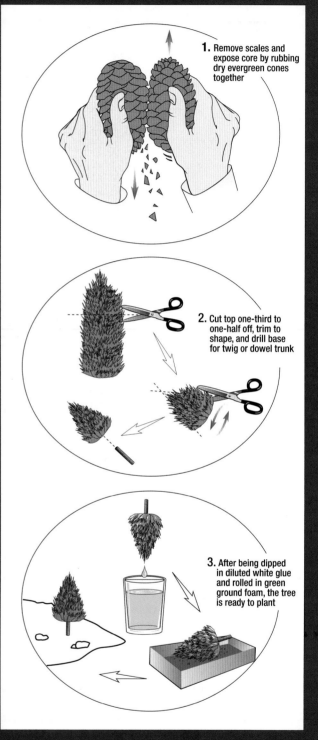

**1.** Remove scales and expose core by rubbing dry evergreen cones together

**2.** Cut top one-third to one-half off, trim to shape, and drill base for twig or dowel trunk

**3.** After being dipped in diluted white glue and rolled in green ground foam, the tree is ready to plant

## Quick background trees

Most model railroads need a surprisingly large number of trees, but the trees don't all need to be detailed models. Several years ago, Jim Kelly used a simple (and cheap) technique to make a lot of treetops to cover the hills of *Model Railroader*'s Turtle Creek Central project layout.

Start with some Woodland Scenics no. 178 green poly fiber, roll it into tree-sized balls, and cement the balls to the layout with white glue. Once the glue dries, spray the poly fiber balls with Woodland Scenics Scenery Cement, and then sprinkle fine green ground foam (leaves) over the treetops. You can add highlights by dusting a lighter shade of green foam on top of the first layer.

Finally, blend the background treetops into your foreground scenery by adding a few complete trees (trunk and branches) in front of the poly fiber balls. To the casual viewer, those few foreground trees will lead them to believe that your entire forest is made up of individual trees.

*(First appeared in* Model Railroader *January 2006)*

## Pine trees from pine cones

Affordable evergreen trees are as close as your nearest real evergreen. Modeler Enrico Scull of Catskill, N.Y., makes convincing scale-model evergreens from Norwegian spruce tree cones. With a little work and a little white glue, ground foam, and wood stain, you can turn out entire model forests at essentially no cost.

After the cones have thoroughly dried, take one in each hand and vigorously rubs the cones together in opposite directions. This removes the scales, and opens the cones to expose the core and surrounding fibers. Cut the cone to size (only the top one-third to one-half of the cone is needed for N or HO scale respectively). Make sure you have a flat base, which you can drill for an appropriately sized trunk. For trunks, you can use twigs or dowels dyed with dark brown wood stain.

Trim the cone into a tree shape, reducing the cone to practically its core in the process. Then dip the entire tree into a mixture of equal parts white glue and water, shake off the excess glue, and roll the tree in Woodland Scenics no. T1345 Green Grass fine ground foam. Some trees may need a second application of glue.

*(First appeared in* Model Railroader *April 2006)*

**2-12**

Brush diluted glue on the underside of the flower head so it is evenly coated.

**2-13**

Apply coarse ground foam to all sides of the flower head.

**2-14**

Sprinkle fine ground foam on top of the coarse foam to fill any gaps and add highlights.

**2-15**

Stand your finished sedum trees in a block of foam for easy drying.

since I model in N scale) is actually a medium-coarse ground foam. I also used Woodland Scenics T1349 Green Blend turf, which is much finer.

To add the leaves, start by dipping the canopy of the tree into white glue diluted 50/50 with water. You can also use diluted matte medium. Use a paintbrush to make sure that the glue evenly covers the underside of the flower head, **2-12**. I also use the brush to remove any excess glue from the armature, as too much glue will cause the foam leaves to run down the branches and stick to the trunk of the tree.

Next, I dip the tree into a container partially filled with the medium-coarse ground foam (Scenic Express). I use this larger ground foam to add some size and airiness to the tree canopy, which also helps to disguise the sedum's flower head. Make sure the foam also covers the underside of the flower head, **2-13**.

After shaking off the loose foam, I then sprinkle the canopy with Woodland Scenics fine green foam, **2-14**. This does two things for the finished tree. First, the finer foam fills in the gaps left between the pieces of medium-coarse foam, and the lighter color adds sun highlights to the top of the tree, giving the leaf canopy some depth.

Once I'm happy with how the tree looks, I set it aside to dry, **2-15**, and then move on to the next one. You can vary the look of your trees by using different shades of ground foam. Looking at real trees for examples of coloration is always a good idea.

## Planting the trees

After the trees have had several hours to dry, I plant them on the layout, plac-

ing the best-looking ones in the foreground where they are the most visible.

Sedum trees are easy to make, although several of the steps require a day each for the materials to dry. To speed things up, you can make the trees in small batches, assembly-line fashion.

On the first night, soak a small batch of sedum stalks in matte medium and let them dry. The second night, assemble and paint the first batch, but also soak a new batch of sedum. By the third night, you can do all of the steps: soaking, assembling, painting, and finishing. After a week or two of this, you should have plenty of great-looking trees for your layout for a fraction of the cost of ready-made trees or tree kits. So what are you waiting for? Next spring plant some sedum!

*(First appeared in* Model Railroader *November 2009)*

CHAPTER THREE    by Mike Confalone

# The mud season of northern New England

This view shows some of the major scenic elements of mud season in northern New England, including melting snow piles and lots of deciduous trees and evergreens, as former B&M S3 no. 1186 enters Woodbury Yard. Trees should dominate the railroad.

Northern New England, which includes the states of Maine, New Hampshire, and Vermont, has five distinct seasons: winter, mud season, spring, summer, and fall. The mud season, or fifth season, occurs between winter and spring in late March and April and is very distinctive in its look, **3-1**. It generally consists of melting snow, leafless trees, swollen rivers, and lots of muddy, wet ground. Successfully modeling this season requires an entirely different approach to scenery. You take some matted spring grass and lots of evergreens and leafless trees, mix in some mud and a few piles of dirty snow, add a photo backdrop, and you've got the makings of a real northern New England mud season.

**3-2**

A hand-made eastern white pine, made from caspia, is featured prominently at right, along with deciduous bare trees made from blueberry bush and SuperTrees materials. Some trees were created by wrapping several branches together with brown floral tape.

**3-3**

This bare deciduous is a good example of a tree made from a sagebrush armature.

**3-4**

Matted spring grass dominates this scene as Alco C420 no. 204 climbs up a sharp grade at Granite Junction. Note the mature tree in the foreground. It is made from sagebrush with some baby's breath sprigs added to the armature.

**3-5**

Piles of dirty, melting snow accumulate in woodyards and other industrial areas. They are made of compressed white floral Styrofoam that is shaped, colored with a wash of thinned paint, and sprinkled with debris.

## Creating trees

In April in northern New England, the trees are still bare, and there is lots of dirty, melting snow lying on matted-down, yellow-brown grass. Without leaves on the deciduous trees, the vast number of evergreen trees in this region is clearly evident. Spruce, eastern white pine and other soft woods dominate the landscape and dwarf the railroad. In order to achieve the right look, the tree-to-track ratio needs to be overwhelmingly in favor of the trees. Just when you think you have made enough trees, make lots more!

Most of my spruce trees are made from Timberline Scenery Products bare tree armatures that I paint and flock with dark-green electrostatic needles. To do this effectively, I spray the armatures with hair spray and then apply the electrostatic needles with a Noch Gras-Master. Using the Gras-Master

allows the spruce needles to stand on end, which gives them a more realistic appearance. This is a more effective way of making evergreen trees as opposed to the standard method of using clumpy ground foam. I also employ some ready-made spruce trees from Heki. Making Eastern white pines is time-consuming, as I construct them branch by branch from caspia, a commercial dried flower found in craft stores, **3-2**. Each trunk is typically made from a straight branch from an actual pine tree or from a pine broom, which can also be found in craft stores. I also use the Gras-Master to flock the caspia pine boughs.

To create realistic leafless, deciduous trees, I handcraft the bare armatures from low-growing blueberry bush or the tips of a natural pine broom. The blueberry bush or other similar low-lying bushes can be found in many wooded areas. Your best bet is to take

a walk in the woods or your backyard and look for suitable tree armatures that have a fine branch structure. The floral section of many craft stores will also yield some usable armatures. You can tie several branches together using brown floral tape to create a larger, denser tree. Another armature option is sagebrush, especially when making older, established trees, **3-3**. Several scenery suppliers offer sagebrush armatures, and they make effective, mature trees when supplemented with fine branches. To fill out a tree, you can hot-glue additional fine branches to the tips of the armatures using another commercial dried flower called gypsophilia, or baby's breath.

## Adding ground cover

For ground cover, I use only real shredded leaves and sifted dirt. Again, a walk through the woods pays

**3-6**

The gravel pit at Granite Junction is made from real rocks, sand, and gravel. Finishing details include tire tracks in the sand and mud and sand on the frond-end loader.

**3-7**

The International Paper woodyard at Grafton Notch occupies a tight corner on my Allagash Railway. The company sign, a simple muddy road, matted grass, a few piles of pulpwood, and a short siding are all that is needed to suggest Maine's big-time wood industry.

**3-8**

In this view of the Prentiss & Carlisle pulpwood yard, you can see the puddles and mud that are typical of a woodyard in early spring. The Minwax Polycrylic provides a wet, muddy look. For a more realistic look, I added wood shavings, dirt, and other debris.

**3-9**

To make a muddy road, spread Durham's water putty, colored grayish brown, to the desired width until it is smooth. Then cover it with a mud mixture, adding ruts and tire tracks.

dividends for finding realistic scenery materials. Simply gather some leaves and put them into a blender with water. Then grind them up, wring out the excess water, and spread them on a cookie sheet. Put the leaves in the oven at 200 degrees for a little while until they are dry and then dry-sift the pieces into various grades. Spread them around your layout, along with sifted dirt and other forest debris, and you've got the makings of a highly realistic forest floor.

Another telltale sign of early spring in northern New England is dead, yellow or brown matted-down grass. It's matted down because it has had snow lying on top of it for six months! I model this effect using a natural product called Tree Branch Fibers from Sweetwater Scenery, **3-4**. Just lay it down, soak it with diluted white glue, and press it into the scenery base.

On top of the matted-down grass are piles of melting snow. This is typical of late March and April, when the warming spring sun begins to take hold and slowly melts away the snow piles. It is important to note that melting snow looks nothing like freshly fallen snow, and modeling this effect proved to be a real challenge. After many false starts, using everything from baking soda to marble dust and everything in between, I finally discovered a solution that gives an extremely realistic effect.

I take small chunks of white floral Styrofoam, compress it between my thumb and forefinger, and glue it right to the ground with hot glue. (For more on this technique, see Chapter Twenty-One.) For high-traffic areas, I discolor it with washes of brown and gray acrylic paints to give it that end-of-season, dirty-snow look. The Styrofoam can also be layered to create deeper piles of

snow for parking lots, industrial areas, and anywhere snow could be plowed into a pile, **3-5**. To form these snow piles, take thin pieces of the Styrofoam and layer them with hot glue. The resulting pile can then be shaped with a saw or other carving tool and colored with a wash of thinned paint.

Except for the Styrofoam snow and a few other details, I use mostly natural scenery materials on my layout. Another natural feature is a gravel pit, which I constructed from real dirt, sand, and crushed stone, **3-6**. I add tile grout to this mix to provide very fine particles and a uniform color. (For more on how the gravel pit was constructed, see the March 2009 issue of *Model Railroader*.)

## Making mud

One of the most important industries on my model railroad is pulpwood processing. On my new Allagash Railway,

**3-10**

Work some mud mixture onto the road to show truck traffic. Use less mud as trucks travel away from the woodyard. Ruts and tire tracks are made into the still-wet mixture with HO scale vehicles. Here, RS10 no. 8587 enters the yard at Granite Junction with loaded woodchip cars.

**3-11**

This view offers a good view of the tree-covered mountains on the realistic photo backdrop. An empty woodchip train approaches the covered bridge at East Wolcott, Vt.

which is set in Maine, there are several pulpwood yards and log yards, **3-7**. A critical feature of early spring in New England is the mud. (Folks actually call it mud season!) Due to the time of year, most of the industrial areas on my model railroad, such as the Prentiss & Carlisle pulpwood yard at Notch Junction, are covered with mud, **3-8**.

Modeling this extremely realistic effect is easy. I put together a mixture of sifted dirt, white glue, a little water, and some dark brown flat latex paint. I mix it to the consistency of barbecue sauce and then spread it around. Using HO scale vehicles (trucks and front-end loaders work great), I run the tires through the mud to create ruts and tire marks. When the surface of the mud-mixture dries, I coat it with Minwax Polycrylic, a latex, satin-finish polyurethane that dries hard and maintains a wet look. While the Polycrylic is still wet, I add wood shavings, dirt, and other debris for a messy, backwoods logging scene.

## Detailing the woodyard

Nothing looks more convincing than natural scenery materials, so I gather dead pine and spruce branches to use as pulpwood logs. I cut the branches with a chop saw to various lengths (generally 4- and 8-foot scale lengths).

Mud puddles are another scenic detail found throughout the woodyard and elsewhere on the layout. I make these from two-part Envirotex epoxy, tinted with a few drops of Polly Scale brown paint. After pouring the mixture

**3-12**

The photo backdrop gives this 12"-wide scene depth. Many fifth-season scenic elements are featured in this scene including bare trees, spruce trees, ground-up leaves, dead spring grass, and a few piles of melting snow.

into crevices or shallow ruts to form reflective puddles, be sure to blow out any bubbles in the epoxy.

And finally, every woodyard needs an access road for logging trucks and other vehicles, **3-9**. My road is made with Durham's water putty mixed to the consistency of pancake batter and colored with grayish brown paint. I spread the Durham's water putty to the desired width with a knife or piece of scrap styrene until it is smooth and level. After the road is almost dry, I sprinkle on fine sifted dirt and work it in with the wheels of HO scale vehicles. To simulate truck traffic, I also work the surrounding, still-wet mud mixture onto the road, using less and less mud as trucks move away from the woodyard, **3-10**.

## Completing the scene

To complement the trees and other scenery, the most important element of all is probably a high-resolution photo backdrop, **3-11**. Employing a photo backdrop behind the foreground scenery expands the apparent depth of the scene and, in my view, is an absolute prerequisite to creating convincing scenery in any season, **3-12**. Placing trees, rocks, and other scenery at the back of the layout reinforces the illusion that a scene continues into the backdrop. Without a photo backdrop, the scene shrinks instantly. A hand-painted backdrop can be effective too but not nearly as realistic as a good-quality photo. For my backdrop, I photographed the wooded mountain areas and other spring scenes of northern New England.

4-1

CHAPTER FOUR    by David Popp

# Water over the dam

**Building impressive water scenes, such as this dam and waterfall, is easier than you may think.**

Water scenes on a model railroad are usually some of the most impressive looking scenery you can make. Small dams are a common feature on rivers, and with a little careful study, they are very easy to build on a model railroad. I recently installed a river scene on my N scale layout that included a dam with water cascading over it, **4-1**. The techniques here can also be used to model waterfalls and fast-moving water, which is common in spring when rivers swell with rain and melting snow and ice.

4-2

This dam along the Fox River in Burlington, Wis., is typical of many dams found along rivers all over the country.

4-3

The dam's wall and foundation are made from simple wood parts that can be cut on a table saw.

4-4

To trim the cast-plaster wing walls, I first removed an end buttress with a razor saw.

4-5

The cut plaster edges clean up easily with a sanding block.

## Constructing the dam

I started the project by first constructing the dam. After doing a little Internet research, I found a photo of a dam on the Naugatuck River in Connecticut that I wanted to model. I was pleased to discover that it was very similar to one along the Fox River in Burlington, Wis., which is near my home, 4-2.

The dam itself is a simple concrete wall having a sloped face set at an approximately 60-degree angle. To make the wall, I cut a wood block with my table saw and then sanded the block smooth. The dam rests on top of a concrete slab foundation. The slab juts out several feet from the bottom. While the Burlington dam's foundation is covered with rock, the Naugatuck River's dam is not, so I had to model the foundation as well as the wall, 4-3.

To make the slab, I cut a small piece of ¼" tempered hardboard. I glued the dam's wall to the foundation with yellow carpenter's glue, and since I needed to get a watertight fit, I clamped the parts for about an hour until the glue dried.

## Building the riverbed

The base for my riverbed is made from ¼" plywood. For the upper riverbed, I attached a piece of ¾" plywood, leaving a ¾" shelf between the two levels.

When assembled, the dam fits in front of the shelf.

The riverbanks are made from 2" foam blocks. I roughly cut the blocks to shape and then sanded them to form the correct slope. I cemented the blocks to the plywood with latex caulk.

The Naugatuck dam has stone wing walls at each end that prevent the river from cutting away the bank on either side and bypassing the dam. For the wing walls on my dam, I used AIM Products plaster retaining-wall castings.

I like working with plaster castings because they are easy to cut and shape. I cut one end buttress from the right wing wall section so that the wing wall for the dam could fit next to the other wall sections I was using to line the right riverbank, 4-4. (If you're not lining the banks with retaining walls, you can skip this step.) The plaster material cuts easily with a razor saw, and I cleaned up the edges with a sanding block, 4-5.

After test-fitting the parts for the dam, I cut the wall and foundation to the correct length. At this time, I also marked the left wing wall, which needed to be shorter than the one on the right, and cut a ¾" notch in it so it would fit between the two levels of the river, 4-6. I then cut openings in the foam bank for the wing walls.

To assemble the dam, I used latex caulk, 4-7. The caulk works well as an adhesive for the plaster, wood, and foam parts, and it provides a good seal between the levels, ensuring that the resin used for the water doesn't leak. While I was at it, I sealed the riverbanks with caulk as well and cemented the dam in place, 4-8.

## Completing the scenery

Once the caulk had dried, it was time to paint the banks, dam, and river bottom and complete the surround-

4-6

The left wing wall needed to be shorter than the one on the right, so I cut the plaster casting to fit between the two river levels.

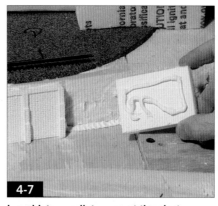

4-7

I used latex caulk to cement the plaster, wood, and foam parts together when installing the right wing wall.

4-8

The caulk provides a watertight seal, keeping the resin from leaking between the two levels. Here is the installed dam before painting.

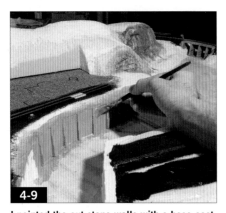

4-9

I painted the cut stone walls with a base coat of Polly Scale Mud and then applied a wash of Mineral Red paint diluted 2:1 with water.

4-10

It's important to finish the surrounding scenery before pouring the resin as scenery cement can seep under the resin and ruin the finish.

4-11

Before pouring the resin, make styrene dams to plug the ends of the riverbed. Seal the seams with clear latex caulk to prevent resin leaks.

ing scenery. I painted the plaster wing walls with Polly Scale Mud, **4-9**. I then flowed on a wash of Polly Scale Mineral Red (one part paint to two parts water) to add some color variations. The wall of the dam is supposed to be concrete, so I painted it Polly Scale Concrete. After the paint dried, I applied an India ink stain (one part ink to ten parts 70 percent isopropyl alcohol) to the dam and wing walls.

I gave the ink several hours to dry before I painted the remaining scenery with tan latex house paint. I then painted the river bottom with flat black latex.

I let the paint dry overnight, and then I applied the surrounding scenery base. It is very important to finish the bulk of the scenery around the riverbed before pouring the resin, **4-10**. Diluted matte medium and other scenery adhesives can easily seep under the resin water and ruin it, so before pouring any resin, make sure you have finished all work near the water that requires adhesives.

For the riverbanks and surrounding scenery base, I used Woodland Scenics earth blend ground foam, followed by some Scenic Express course turf in several darker colors. I then soaked everything liberally with diluted matte medium (one part matte medium to one part water) and applied Woodland Scenics fine static grass using a Noch Gras-Master applicator.

I lined the riverbed with a blend of several different sizes of Woodland Scenics gray talus. I covered most of the bed in front of the dam with talus, as a river's current often exposes the bare rock at the base of a dam.

## Pouring the resin

After the scenery was finished, I used styrene strips to plug the ends of the river, so the resin wouldn't escape. I taped the styrene to the edge of the scene, **4-11**, and then sealed the interior seams with clear latex caulk.

Once the caulk had dried, I mixed the first batch of Magic Water by Unreal Details (www.unrealdetails.com). This material comes with detailed instructions and is easy to use. I poured the river in several layers, approximately ⅛" at a time, **4-12**.

Before pouring the first layer or resin, I tinted it with a small amount of Floquil Railroad Tie brown (you need an organic solvent-based paint for this) to give it that murky river-water look, **4-13**. Let the material harden (usually 30 hours or so) before pouring the next layer.

For the second layer, I used about half the amount of Floquil paint, and the final layer had no paint at all. This technique makes the resin water seem deeper than it really is.

## Adjusting the dam

After evaluating the first resin pour, I realized that the wall of the dam was taller than I wanted, and it was going to take a lot of resin to fill the upper river. I

4-12

The resin needs to be poured in layers. This photo shows the first ⅛" layer.

4-13

I tinted the initial layer with Floquil Railroad Tie Brown to add a sense of depth and river color.

4-14

After pouring the first layer of resin, I decided to lower the dam by cutting a spillway into the top using a razor saw and wood chisel.

4-15

To make the waterfall, I brushed two layers of Woodland Scenics Water Effects material on a sheet of glass. I tinted the second layer with Polly Scale Railroad Tie Brown to match the color of the river water.

adjusted the height of the dam by cutting a spillway into the top of the wall, **4-14**. I formed the spillway by first making two ⅛" deep cuts into the top of the wall. I then used a ½" wood chisel to remove the material between the cuts. After sanding the cut smooth, I painted the exposed wood surface Polly Scale Concrete.

With the spillway added, I then resumed pouring resin until the water level behind the dam was just below the top of it.

## Water over the dam

Next came the best part, making the water flow over the dam. For this

step, I used Woodland Scenics Water Effects, a paste-like substance that dries clear and remains flexible. To make the waterfall, I placed some of the Water Effects material on a sheet of glass, **4-15**. (You can use almost any solid, nonstick surface.) I then used a paintbrush to work the material so that it had lines that ran parallel. Once the first application of Water Effects had dried, I added a second coat. With this coat, I mixed in a bit of the same color paint I used for tinting the resin, but this time I used the acrylic version, Polly Scale Railroad Tie Brown, as the Water Effects material is water-soluble.

Once the second layer dried, I cut the sheet of Water Effects to the size needed to cover the dam. Then, after removing all the surrounding material, I carefully pried up the edge of the waterfall and gently peeled it off the glass, **4-16**.

After testing to make sure it would fit, I coated the top of the dam and the top of the foundation with more Water Effects and set the waterfall in place, **4-17**. Once the waterfall had a day to dry, I poured the final layer of resin on the upper level of the river, bringing the water's surface even with the top of the waterfall.

4-16

After cutting away the excess material, gently remove the waterfall from the glass and apply it to the dam.

4-17

I cemented the waterfall to the dam with more Water Effects and let it dry.

4-18

I added the waves to the lower river using more Water Effects. The material goes on white but dries clear.

4-19

After the waterfall and waves dry, use white paint to create foam on the wave tops and in the falls.

4-20

The local switcher works its way north past the completed dam at Torrington, Conn., on my N scale Naugatuck Valley RR.

I also used the Water Effects material to create an area of turbulent water beyond the dam, thinning out the larger waves the farther they get from the falls, **4-18**. After this layer of Water Effects dried, I added some foam highlights, using white paint, to the falling water as well as to the water at the bottom of the falls, **4-19**.

## Anyone can do it

Drying times are the slowest part of this project. While it will take more than a week of evenings to complete a water scene like this one, the end results are well worth the effort. And once the project is finished, **4-20**, you'll have an exciting river scene that will be one of the highlights of your model railroad.

5-1

CHAPTER FIVE    by Mike Danneman

# Spring backdrop tips

Representing springtime on your backdrop is easy. The important thing to remember is to use the same spring foliage colors and tones on the backdrop that you use on your scenery, **5-1**. Sometimes, springtime can seem like it takes forever to arrive after the icy grip of a long winter, **5-2**. And after it arrives, early spring colors can differ from those in late spring.

**In this view on my N scale Rio Grande Moffat Road, a freight led by two GP30s and a Tunnel Motor exits Tunnel 1. The backdrop behind the rear of the train, representing the mouth of Coal Creek Canyon, is 7 feet away from the locomotives. Careful color selection on the painted backdrop matches the ground cover as closely as possible, which allows for a seamless view.**

5-2

Springtime comes earlier in the season in some locales. At Sandcut, Calif., a Southern Pacific westbound curves through the green scenery. Air inversions frequently invade this area in spring, creating hazy mountain backgrounds for trains. Reproducing this on a backdrop would go a long way in nicely representing the season and, more importantly, distance.

5-3

In parts of the West, spring can still be dry. This BNSF coal train threads through scenic Wendover Canyon in Wyoming on May 25, 1997. The only hints of spring can be seen in the colors of the shrubs and trees at river's edge. The grasses sure don't scream spring! The distant mountains have the same color textures. When adding backdrops to such scenes, try to match the tones of scenery materials like the grasses and trees.

5-4

A Norfolk Southern train leaves Danville, Ky., northbound on May 18, 1994. By this date, the trees are in their green splendor, and the grasses in the surrounding fields have yet to feel the scorching rays of a hot summer sun. The tree lines in the background would look very nice painted on the backdrop, with some of the fields serving as transition areas.

5-5

A BNSF stack train heads east over Marias Pass in Montana on June 4, 2002. The amount of snow lingering on the surrounding peaks would make a dramatic addition to mountains on a springtime backdrop.

If you are modeling very early spring, many of the grassy areas might still be brown or just beginning to turn green, 5-3. Early spring trees will begin to bud out and have a very spring-green color, so extend these same spring-green colors to your backdrop, 5-4. Make sure you keep the backdrop scenery more subdued and slightly lighter in color to suggest distance. Don't be afraid to touch up colors on your backdrop at anytime during the layout-building process.

If you are modeling mountainous areas of the West, many of the higher peaks are still shrouded in snow or at least contain numerous patchy snow-

fields, 5-5. By adding these snow effects to the higher mountains, you will be representing springtime in the Rockies, as by mid to late summer, much or all of this snow will be melted. Dabbing titanium white acrylic paint in a random manner onto finished mountain peaks nicely represents these snow patches. For placement, think about where the snow would gather, such as in the low crevasses and talus slopes between peaks. To add some shadows and give the stark white a cooler color, you can mix in a very small amount of sky blue.

Another indication that your backdrop represents springtime is a

random thunderstorm brewing on the horizon. By using various tones of titanium white and sky blue, mixed with small amounts of Payne's Gray for shadows, a nice likeness of a thunderhead can be painted. While painting one on your backdrop, it's a good idea to look through some photographs of thunderstorms to see how they form and are shaped. When a storm is high enough in the atmosphere, an anvil-shaped head will sometimes appear. Be careful when painting these unique shapes on the backdrop, as they may not look very realistic if the forms are too unbelievable, 5-6.

**5-6**

Over North Yard, a spring thunderstorm brews to the west. Note the well-defined shape of the storm cloud with the anvil-shaped top, which is commonly associated with Western thunderstorms. Try not to overdo it with these distinct shapes though, as they tend to draw focus.

**5-7**

A gathering thunderstorm to the north frames a westbound UP train at Kyune, Utah on May 21, 2002. A good-sized thunderstorm need not have a definitive shape on a backdrop. A layered and dark expansive underside of a storm might just do the trick to represent such weather phenomenon.

**5-8**

In the mountains of Colorado, it always snows in the springtime. At Pinecliffe, another snowstorm approaches from the west. Note how the expansive storm clouds don't have a specific shape to them because of their size.

**5-9**

Spring clouds can sometimes be dense, such as these seen above a BNSF coal train near Alliance, Neb., on June 14, 1998. On a sky backdrop, areas of thick clouds mixed with patches of clear sky offer a more realistic look.

You can create the effect of rain falling from a cloud by mixing a very small amount of Payne's Gray with water and applying it with a large brush. Make sure this paint mixture is thin and colorless so that it acts like a wash. Lightly paint this thin wash from the undersides of the clouds to the ground to produce rain shafts. You can also let these wispy shafts end in the sky underneath the cloud to show virga, a rain that never reaches the ground, which is fairly common in the dry regions of the West.

A more substantial storm can be painted on your backdrop by using various shades of grays to represent approaching storm clouds, **5-7**. If you have a darker region of your layout due to your lighting configuration, a storm on the backdrop in this area might be a good idea instead of adding more lighting.

On one part of my layout, I have a gray sky representing a brewing storm. The town of Pinecliffe is cloaked in snow from a passing storm, **5-8**. Remember, in the higher elevations of the West, it can, and frequently does, snow heavily in the springtime. So another wave of stormy, snowy weather nears the town. The gray clouds do not have a well-

defined shape and are feathered into the blue sky on the left-hand side of the scene. Feel free to not only add clouds to your backdrop, but you can make the backdrop mostly cloudy, **5-9**. Springtime often means precipitation, so cloud-filled, stormy, or even overcast skies are appropriate for a springtime backdrop.

When painting a spring backdrop on your layout, think of the season's colors and textures and how they are different than in summer. Summer may be the most modeled season, but with some subtle changes, you can depict a growing green season that awakens after the slumber of winter.

# Modeling summer

## by Lance Mindheim

On a summer day in August 1976, northbound Illinois Central Gulf train IM-2 crosses the Shuffle Creek viaduct in Unionville, Ind. Everything is green on the surrounding hills but not the same shade. *Photo by Lance Mindheim*

If you ask somebody what images come to mind when you throw out the word *summer*, the first responses will likely be sunny blue skies, Fourth of July celebrations, and balmy weather. But summer isn't a uniform season. It is characterized by a graduated range of colors and textures that vary substantially depending on location and time of the season. Early summer in many places is characterized by verdant, emerald-green foliage that seems on the verge of swallowing every man-made object in its path. A month later, after a succession of scorching hot days, the grass will start to brown and may be so brittle it crunches beneath your feet.

Across the country, a summer day can vary greatly. Summer treats Maine residents to sapphire blue skies, moderate temperatures, low humidity, and endless trains of white, puffy clouds parading across the sky. In the Midwest, moments after stepping outside, the temperature and humidity, both in the 90s, can make your shirt stick to your back. In the Rocky Mountains of Colorado, you could be greeted with a wintery blast of snow and cold.

When reflecting upon summer weather, we generally think of sunny skies, but summer also brings rain and thunderstorms. Just as winter features days of blue sunny skies, summer has its share of gray days. Often, even on cloudless days, the elements combine to serve up a sky of lackluster grayish brown haze.

Summer vegetation takes on a broad variety of colors, shapes, and textures. Even on the same tree, leaves can sparkle in different shades of green. Green foliage can have different levels of blue or yellow tints. Weeds love summer, and they may completely obscure the base of a tree. They can have single stalks or be sprawling low-lying canopies and have a touch of color from sprouting flowers. Grass may be dark green if treated to a good season of rain, or it may be beige in a particularly dry year. Grass next to a right-of-way may be completely brown, killed off by the maintenance-of-way crew's weed sprayer.

One of the most pleasing aspects of nature is the random patterns that occur. It is rare to look at a line of trees and see each one the same height, variety, and distance apart. By nature, we are creatures of order, and it often takes a conscious effort to create random patterns when we place vegetation on our model railroads. Instilling such randomness is worth the effort though. If we can carry it off, we have a realistic rendition of the great outdoors.

The variety of scenery products on the market now is at an all-time high. Use this to your advantage. Pick four, five, or six different shades to work with. Vary your tree height and shape. Work different types of foliage around each other. Strive for random patterns. Experiment with different brands and types of scenery products.

So if you set your model railroad in summer, make a point of walking outside and taking in the broad range of greens in nature's color palette. Note the different shapes and textures of the surrounding vegetation and grass beneath your feet. The extra time observing Mother Nature and applying it to your modeling will not only create more realistic results but can also be a quite relaxing pastime in itself.

6-1

Photos by the author

CHAPTER SIX    by Lance Mindheim

# Orderly tree lines and fence lines

As a species, we humans like order in our lives. We like right angles and borders around the structural elements we create or come in contact with. When we landscape our homes, we love orderly arrangements of vegetation and clear delineations of our property boundaries. This desire for order carries over to the scenic landscape and thus to the scenes that frequently appear on our model railroads. Two of the most common borders that appear in nature are tree lines and fence lines. Fence lines are certainly man-made and generally run in straight lines and right angles. Tree lines can be either man-made or natural. As is the case with fences, man-made tree lines are generally linear and run at right angles, **6-1**. Naturally occurring tree lines follow the surrounding geography, **6-2**.

A Monon local heads across southern Indiana past fields that are neatly framed by tree lines and fence lines.

6-2

On August 20, 1977, the southbound *Floridian* rolls through the landscape near Harrodsburg, Ind. Note the tree lines framing the surrounding fields and the meandering tree line paralleling Monroe County's Clear Creek just behind the train.

Use tree line to screen transition from layout to backdrop

Backdrop

Continue tree line between track and backdrop

Partial tree line with breaks

Angle tree line with respect to fascia

Put a few breaks in the trees here

Fascia

6-3

Tree lines, in particular, serve a number of useful purposes for the model railroader from the aesthetic to the practical. Aesthetically, tree lines create a sense of realism and order. On the practical side, tree lines are very handy as visual screens. As screens, tree lines can separate scenes or perhaps hide track we don't want viewers to see.

Fence lines don't have the mass to accomplish what a tree line can. They are, however, something that occurs with such frequency that they should be modeled. In addition, model fence lines give the same sense of boundary as they do in real life.

## Using tree lines

Let's take a look at tree lines first. As mentioned, they are either man-made or naturally occurring. While you will certainly encounter tree lines in urban areas, the most likely place you will see them in a railroad setting will be in the agricultural fields that surround the right-of-way. Often, agricultural fields are laid out in a series of rectangular shapes, 6-3. Many fields are framed by tree lines for various reasons. They could separate one property from the next or one crop field from another. The borders between fields may exist simply because a plow can't get into the area, and trees naturally grow where a plow cannot reach. Or they may be planted around a farmer's residence as a windbreak.

Not all tree lines run in straight lines or at right angles. They also occur

naturally. Streams and creeks attract vegetation, and you can't run a plow right up to the rim of those waterways. As a result, waterways, from large rivers to the tiniest creeks, are generally bordered by trees. In the case of smaller waterways, the bordering trees may be so dense and large in relation to the stream that they totally obscure it. In this instance, you can simply suggest the existence of a small creek by creating a meandering tree line, 6-4.

Modeling a tree line is not so much about modeling individual trees but how those trees are arranged and placed on the layout. Man-made tree lines should be laid out in linear fashion. Run straight tree lines across your layout to frame the fields. At most, the lines should only be one or two trees wide. Added interest can be created if you run the lines at slight angles to the fascia. To the extent possible, run your man-made tree lines parallel or at right angles to each other.

Naturally occurring tree lines are shaped by the geographic elements they border. For example, if you are bordering a creek, you will want the line to follow the creek's banks, 6-5. When a creek runs through an agricultural field, a farmer will want to run his fields as close as possible to the creek, so again, only make your tree line one or two trees wide.

When laying out the tree line, giving a few areas specific attention can go a long way toward enhancing the

sense of realism, 6-6. While the line of trees itself may be straight, you want to break up the uniformity within that line. Introduce random heights of trees. Although the trees may be all green, use different shades of green to break things up. Mix up the species of trees and their associated unique shapes. This includes random evergreens. Some tree lines are also older than others, and an older tree line will have larger trees while a younger tree line has shorter trees. Add an occasional break in the tree line. Work hard to have uneven spacing between trunks. This isn't always easy to do, but you don't want to have the look of evenly spaced trees as they would line a pristine country club boulevard. Finally, it is likely that the trunks of the trees will be concealed by low-lying brush and vegetation, so work that element in around the base of the trees.

## Representing evergreens

Most Eastern and Midwestern tree lines will be composed primarily of deciduous trees. There will however, be an occasional evergreen in the mix. Inserting one into the tree line here and there can add interest and break up the uniformity. When we think of evergreens, thoughts often turn to towering pines out West or perhaps the proverbial Christmas tree. In reality, evergreens come in all shapes and sizes and are found all over the United States. In addition to the more

**6-4** Laying your tree line out in a meandering path suggests the existence of small creek without actually modeling the water.

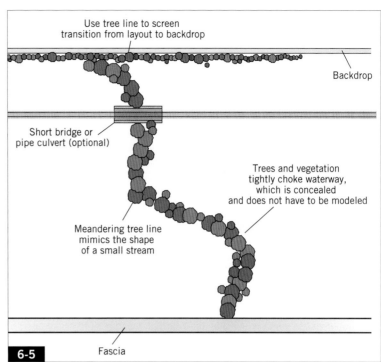

Use tree line to screen transition from layout to backdrop

Backdrop

Short bridge or pipe culvert (optional)

Trees and vegetation tightly choke waterway, which is concealed and does not have to be modeled

Meandering tree line mimics the shape of a small stream

**6-5** Fascia

**6-6** When constructing a tree line, mix in a variety of tree heights and shapes and avoid uniform spacing between the trees. Also, work bushes and weeds up against the trunks of the trees.

**6-7** While SuperTrees armatures are generally associated with deciduous trees, they can also be shaped to make reasonable representations of evergreens.

stately pines and blue spruces, other varieties are relatively short and really quite ratty in appearance. Profiles vary from the traditional conical shape to rounder egg shapes. Heights range from several feet tall to more than 100 feet tall. Colors also vary, ranging from greenish blue to a yellowish lime green.

A plausible representation of a typical, short weedy evergreen can be quickly manufactured using SuperTrees armatures. When mixing evergreens into tree lines, I generally focus on the shorter variety. Select a SuperTrees armature with a straight trunk that is 2" or 3" tall. Give it the shape of the evergreen species of your choice with a scissors and then paint the armature with dark gray auto primer. To add needles, give your painted armature a few puffs of hairspray and sprinkle on short (2mm) green static grass flock, **6-7**. Woodland Scenics dark green (no. FL636) and medium green (no. FL635) work well for this purpose.

## Concealing layout elements

In addition to the aesthetic uses, tree lines can also have practical uses. Their dense nature makes them an ideal screen to conceal elements much in the same manner as a structure would. If you have a small staging yard, consider hiding it behind a screen of thick trees instead of hiding it under the layout on a separate level. If you have two scenes on your layout that are closer together than you would like, run a tree line between them to create a sense of distance.

Tree-line screens can also be handy in hiding the point where the layout meets the backdrop, **6-8**. They can conceal the end of a waterway that disappears in the distance or hide the point where a roadway meets a backdrop.

**6-8**

Thick tree lines are effective in hiding the transition from layout to backdrop as illustrated in this scene from my East Rail layout.

**6-9**

Fence lines often parallel a railroad right-of-way. Here, short vegetation has started to envelop the fencerow in a few locations.

**6-10**

I stained these posts with washes of Floquil Roof Brown, SP Lettering Gray, and Grimy Black. Simple jigs help keep the post height uniform, and a piece of tape marked with post spacing keeps fence lines straight.

## Constructing fence lines

When it comes to creating framing boundaries, a distant cousin to the tree line is the fence line. As with the tree line, the fence line can be used to frame a scene and break up uniform expanses. Obviously it cannot be used to conceal anything as a tree line can. Fence lines are often found parallel to a right-of-way or at field edges, **6-9**. As with tree lines, more visual interest is created if you run the fence line at a slight angle to your layout's fascia.

As to the dimensions of typical fence components, my friend and go-to guy on farming matters, Nelson Cecarelli of Cecarelli Farms, says that they vary depending on the type of agriculture. A typical livestock fence would have posts 4 to 5 feet tall spaced 10 feet apart. Posts in the Northeast are commonly made from cedar or locust trees since these trees are readily available and

would last 15 to 20 years. Some 4 x 4 posts are used in this region but the cost is high. Posts are strung with three or four strands of barbed wire and possibly one strand of electric wire. Horse farms and hobby farms tend to use a pressure-treated 4 x 4 posts.

When modeling a fence, it is important to consider how you will model the wire itself. If a material, such as fence wire, is not available in scale model dimensions, you are better off not using it and letting your imagination fill things in. This applies, in particular, to model fence wire that is often oversize. Trying to model a wire mesh fence with the oversize materials that are presently available creates something that is highly distracting visually. You are far better off modeling the posts and leaving the wire off.

I don't get too scientific when modeling agricultural fences. The materials

for modeling a fence line are relatively basic: dimensional lumber and solvent-based paints in gray and brown tones. I use scale lumber to represent the appropriate 4 x 4 or 6 x 6 posts. I stain the posts a driftwood gray or dark brown using solvent-based paints and insert them in the scenery at scale 10-foot intervals, **6-10**. When gluing, try to keep the posts vertical. A simple jig will help you keep the fence posts a uniform height, and a piece of tape marked at uniform intervals helps align the posts.

Tree lines and fence lines are simple, yet highly effective, tools for creating a sense of realism. They replicate the natural and man-made boundaries that occur frequently in the areas surrounding our railroads. In addition, they can be excellent visual screens, scene separators, and transition pieces.

7-1

Photos by the author and Dorothy Grivno

CHAPTER SEVEN    by Cody Grivno

# Corn on the strip and other crops

Corn of some variety is grown in most states, and nothing typifies a summer crop better than a green and growing cornfield. Especially if your layout is set in the Midwest, odds are you'll need a cornfield or two for your model railroad, **7-1**.

Various methods for modeling corn have included the use of asparagus fern, artificial turf, and brass etchings. After German manufacturer Busch came out with injection-molded plastic cornfield kits (no. 1202), I decided to give them a try. A kit contains 20 rows of corn, each having 20 crisply molded, 1" tall stalks that are detailed right down to the tiny ears of corn. The kit also includes a small packet of fine ground foam for simulating tassels on the top of each stalk.

**Cornfields, ditches, culverts, and farm roads are common throughout the Midwest. Follow the techniques I used for modeling this rural scene.**

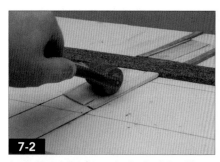

**7-2**

Apply latex adhesive to the back of the shims. To ensure that the adhesive bonds evenly to the foam, run a wallpaper roller over the shims.

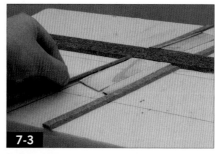

**7-3**

Strips of N scale cork roadbed are used to model the edge of the road. These strips also serve as a guide for positioning the ditches.

**7-4**

Let the latex adhesive dry for a day, then blend the wood shims and cork strips with Sculptamold, which is great for scenery work.

**7-5**

To give the ditch bottom a U shape, a medium-grit sanding block with a rounded edge works well.

**7-6**

After installing, blend the culverts into the scenery with Sculptamold. I made the culvert following Rand Hood's article in the March 1997 issue of *Model Railroader*.

**7-7**

Dark brown paint works well as an undercoating for ditch bottoms and fields.

With 400 plants, a Busch cornfield covers a 4" square area. Unfortunately, modeling a field that looks bigger than a garden requires space—and lots of it. Purchasing six, eight, or more cornfield kits can be expensive. That's where the aisle comes into play. By planting a field at the layout's edge, you can suggest that the scenery continues into the aisle without actually modeling it. Follow along as I show you how to model a cornfield along a layout's edge.

## Getting started

I built my diorama's base from 2"-thick extruded-foam insulation board. This material is easy to cut and shape, and it takes acrylic and latex paint well. (Don't use solvent-based paints or adhesives as they will dissolve the foam.) I planned out a rural area that included a farm with cattle and cornfields.

I started with the track and attached HO scale cork roadbed with DAP Dynaflex 230 latex adhesive. Installing the roadbed first gave me a point of reference for laying out the roads, ditches, and culverts.

With the roadbed in place, I laid out the road. Many of the gravel farm roads I traveled on during my youth in rural Minnesota had a slight incline as they approached the tracks at grade. To re-create this feature, I cut wood shims to match the height of the roadbed. I secured the shims to the foam with latex adhesive, **7-2**. Then I pressed the adhesive-coated shims into place with a wallpaper roller to form a strong bond.

I used N scale cork strips to establish the edge of the road, **7-3**. The edges of the cork serve as a guide when I later shaped the ditch profiles. I attached the cork with latex adhesive, and let it dry for 24 hours before proceeding, **7-4**.

The next day, I seamlessly blended the shims and cork using Sculptamold, a papier-mâché-like material. Since this is a gravel road, I didn't try to make the Sculptamold perfectly level. Most real gravel farm roads are far from smooth.

## Shaping ditches

You can use a variety of tools to cut and shape foam, including hot wire foam cutters, heated knives, wire brushes, and razor knives. For cutting out the ditch profile, I used a razor knife.

Then, I gave the ditch its basic shape with a coarse-grit, sponge-rubber sand-

ing block. I didn't sand right to the edge of the HO scale cork roadbed in order to leave a transition area between the edge of the ballast and the tall ditch grass.

Next, I used a medium-grit, round-edge block to give the ditch its final shape, **7-5**. I found that the sanding blocks worked best when I made light, smooth passes. If I applied too much pressure, they had a tendency to dig into the foam and tear it out in chunks.

After shaping the ditches, I looked over the diorama. I wasn't happy with the elevation of the field in relationship to the road and the railroad right-of-way. To fix this problem, I removed a ⅛" layer of foam from the field with a Stanley Surform tool. I kept a shop vacuum handy during this step. The foam dust is attracted to static electricity, so before long, my tools, work surface, and clothes were covered in pink dust. Whenever the Surform became filled with foam shavings, I stopped to vacuum the diorama and the surrounding area.

A ditch wouldn't be complete without culverts. Since I didn't have any in my scenery supply box, I decided to make my own. I formed Campbell corrugated aluminum (no. 802) into scale

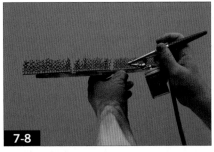

**7-8**

For a final color, paint the corn stalks Polly Scale Reading Green.

**7-9**

When you have many corn strips to tassel, it is easier to dip them first in Woodland Scenics Scenic Cement (left) and then in Woodland Scenics Yellow Grass fine turf.

**7-10**

After coating the back of each strip with latex adhesive, press them into place with a pair of tweezers. A .080" x .156" styrene strip keeps the rows evenly spaced.

**7-11**

Sprinkling Soil fine turf over the field hides the strip bases, making it appear as though the corn sprouted right from the ground.

**7-12**

Use a pair of smooth-jaw needlenose pliers to twist the stalks into a realistic shape.

**7-13**

Pot toppers have great applications, such as ditch grass, on model train layouts. The material can be attached with white glue.

24"-diameter pipes. It's important to shape the aluminum in light, repeated passes. If you try to shape the aluminum in one or two passes, you'll damage the corrugation detail.

I finished the ditches by filling in rough spots with Sculptamold, **7-6**. To help blend the Sculptamold seamlessly into the foam, I blotted it with a damp sponge. Make sure the sponge isn't too wet; otherwise, it will slow the drying time of the Sculptamold.

## Painting

Using extruded-foam insulation board has one drawback. If you miss a spot when adding scenery, you'll end up with pink or light blue patches underneath the ground foam. To reduce the likelihood of this, I painted the foam with earth-colored flat latex paints. (Any flat earth-tone tan and brown will work.) Before applying the paint, I made sure the latex adhesive and Sculptamold were dry. If you paint over wet adhesive or Sculptamold, they won't dry completely.

Using a foam brush, I first painted the entire foam surface tan. This was a

perfect base color for the roads, but it wouldn't look convincing in the ditches or under the cornfield. I went back and painted these areas dark brown, **7-7**.

## Planting corn on the strip

With the foam scenery base prepared, I turned my attention to the star of the show, the cornfield. I cut the strips from the carrier with sprue cutters and sprayed the strips with Rust-Oleum gray Automobile Primer. When spraying, work in a well-ventilated area and wear safety gear.

After letting the primer dry for 24 hours, I applied the final colors. I airbrushed the complete strips with Polly Scale Reading Green. Once that color dried, I sprayed the bases with Polly Scale Dirt, **7-8**. Don't worry about getting overspray on the base of the corn stalks. It makes them look realistic.

Although Busch includes a small packet of ground foam with each kit to simulate tassels, I didn't feel there was enough for all the strips, so I used Woodland Scenics Yellow Grass fine turf, which is close in color and texture.

I was planting two cornfield kits, so I had 40 strips to tassel. With this large

number of strips, I set up an assembly line to apply the ground foam. I filled one container with Woodland Scenics Scenic Cement (diluted white glue would also work) and the other with Yellow Grass. I first dipped the top 1/8" of the strip in the Scenic Cement. Then I quickly transferred it into the turf, **7-9**. This technique works best before you twist the corn stalks.

Next, I planted the corn rows. I applied a thin layer of latex adhesive to the back of each strip and pressed the strips into place with a tweezers, **7-10**. As I placed the rows, I kept them evenly spaced using a strip of .080" x .156" styrene. This spacing is wider than most rows are planted in a conventional cornfield; however, corn planted in test plots is often spaced wider than normal to better show off its attributes. For the sake of argument, we'll just say these are test plots.

After letting the latex adhesive dry thoroughly (two days), I sprinkled Woodland Scenics Soil fine turf over the field, **7-11**. Then I used a pump sprayer to wet the foam with 70 percent isopropyl alcohol. (You can also use "wet water"—water with a few drops of dish

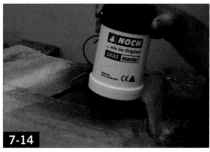

**7-14**

Noch and Woodland Scenics static grass make the turnaround along the perimeter of the cornfield look slightly overgrown.

**7-15**

To add grass along the right-of-way, cut a Faller Wild Grass Meadow sheet into strips and attach them along the edge of the ballast with full-strength white glue.

**7-16**

A soft-bristled toothbrush can tease grass fibers upward, so they do not look as if they are growing at an angle.

**7-17**

Rustic fence posts can be made from lengths of 4 x 4 stripwood stained with an India ink wash. Panel nails, spaced on 8-foot centers, are used to make pilot holes for the posts.

**7-18**

Along the perimeter of the cow pasture, Polly Scale Railroad Tie Brown gives the fence wire a rusted look.

**7-19**

The crossing planks of this rural grade crossing are scale 16-foot lengths of 4 x 8 stripwood.

soap added). This makes it easier for the Scenic Cement to wick its way through the foam. I used a pipette to apply the cement between the rows.

Finally, I twisted the individual corn stalks with a pair of smooth-jaw needle-nose pliers, **7-12**. I twisted the stalks in an alternating pattern, so they all wouldn't face the same direction. Since twisting several hundred individual corn stalks didn't seem that appealing, I skipped a few in the middle of each row.

## Modeling the edge of a field

For better viewing and access, I didn't run the corn rows right up to the edge of the ditch. Instead, I left a 2" unplanted turnaround area around the perimeter of the field. Before I scenicked this area, I installed tall ditch grass using reversible pot toppers, **7-13**. I also used this material to model the cow pastures on the opposite side of the field.

Pot toppers, used for artificial flower displays, are available at Michaels craft stores. Offered in 4" and 6" sizes (no. 412810, 412811), the reversible discs have static grass on one side, brown sawdust on the other, and are filled

with polyfiber. I only needed the static grass side, so I split the pot topper open and removed the sawdust and as much of the polyfiber filling as possible. I then cut the static grass part into strips and attached them with full-strength white glue, using T-pins to hold them in place.

Next, I scenicked the area between the pot-topper grass and the cornfield. I first brushed the turnaround with diluted white glue (80 percent glue and 20 percent water). While the glue was still wet, I randomly sprinkled on Woodland Scenics Burnt Grass, Earth Blend, Soil, and Yellow Grass turf. After the glue dried, I vacuumed up the excess and then applied a second layer of each type of foam to fill in any bare spots. After spraying the second application of foam with isopropyl alcohol, I soaked the area with Scenic Cement.

With the Scenic Cement still wet, I used the Noch Gras-Master to apply Woodland Scencis medium green static flock and a blend of Noch Summer Meadow and Reed Meadow wild grass, **7-14**. The Woodland Scenic static grass fibers are about shin high

on an HO scale figure, and the Noch fibers are approximately waist high. Combining the two simulates the look of a slightly overgrown but not unkempt area. Though static grass is fun to use and looks realistic, it's messy, so place damp paper towels over the adjacent scenery to keep wayward fibers out of those areas.

I finished the scene by sprinkling in light green, dark green, and Yellow Grass coarse turf from Woodland Scenics. This adds yet another texture to the scenery at the field's edge.

## Scenicking the right-of-way

Okay, you may be asking, "Why does scenicking the right-of-way matter?" Well, I needed to add grass to the other side of the ditch along the edge of the ballast. For this step, I used Faller no. 180465 Wild Grass Meadow. Though the scenery material has a self-adhesive backing, I attached it to the diorama with full-strength white glue, **7-15**. I used this same material, as well as Busch Summer Grass (no. 1303) and Late Summer Grass (no. 1304) along the edge of the road.

**7-20**

Fill in the planks with Highball Products N scale limestone ballast to add gravel for the road and then soak it with Scenic Cement.

**7-21**

Drybrushing static grass additional colors gives it a more realistic appearance. Here, Polly Scale Dirt simulates the high-water line by the ditch.

**7-22**

Pouring Realistic Water from a disposable cup instead of pouring it straight from the bottle gives you better control of the product.

**7-23**

The Realistic Water dried to a glass-like finish, which didn't look prototypical. To suggest that the water is flowing, apply a thin layer of Water Effects with a ½" paintbrush.

Though I was happy with the appearance of the wild grass meadow, I wanted the fibers to stand upright and not look like they were growing out of the ditch at an angle. To achieve this look, I teased the fibers upward with a soft-bristled toothbrush, working from the bottom of the ditch to the top, **7-16**. This wasn't a perfect solution, but it did help.

With the grass in place, I next added fence posts, which I cut from 4 x 4 stripwood, **7-17**. I stained the posts with an India ink wash (two teaspoons ink to one pint 70 percent isopropyl alcohol). As the stain was drying, I pressed 1⅝" panel nails into the foam on scale 8-foot centers. Once the stain dried, I dipped the bottom of each post in white glue, removed the nail, and then pressed the stripwood into the opening.

To add a touch of realism to the fence on the pasture side of the tracks, I used Pro Tech Pro Line Pole Line to simulate wire. Though stringing wire sounds difficult, it's actually not. I wrapped the line around the end post and secured it with cyanoacrylate adhesive (CA). I then put a small dot of Woodland Scenics Scenic Accent glue on the back of the intermediate posts and wrapped the elastic line around each one. When I reached the end of the fence line, I again used CA to attach the Pro Line Pole Line. To make the wire look rusty, I applied Polly Scale Railroad Tie Brown with a Microbrush, **7-18**.

## Adding a rural grade crossing

I then turned my attention to the grade crossing. My inspiration for this single-lane grade crossing came from *Soo Line Standards: Vol. 3* published by the Soo Line Historical & Technical Society. I cut two scale 16-foot lengths of 4 x 8 stripwood and stained them with the same India ink wash I used on the fence posts, **7-19**. Once the stain dried, I attached the stripwood to the outside and the gauge side of the rail with medium viscosity CA. To make the bond almost instantaneous, I applied CA accelerator with a Microbrush.

Then I used Highball Products N scale limestone ballast to fill in the area between the planks, **7-20**. First, I sprinkled the ballast into thinned white glue that I had brushed between the planks. When the glue dried, I vacuumed up the excess granules and applied more ballast until it was level with the tops of the planks, keeping it out of the flangeways.

Next, I sprayed the ballast with isopropyl alcohol and let it soak in for a minute. The alcohol breaks the surface tension of the ballast, making it easier for the Scenic Cement to wick through the granules. Using a pipette to apply the Scenic Cement, I knew the ballast was thoroughly saturated once I could see white between the granules.

I let the Scenic Cement dry overnight before weathering the ballast with an airbrush. To simulate grease and oil drippings between the rails, I used thinned Polly Scale Steam Power Black (four parts 70 percent isopropyl alcohol to one part paint). Then, I applied Polly Scale Dirt, thinned at the same ratio, along the edge of the ballast. Weathering the edge of the right-of-way softens the transition between the ballast and the tall grass.

## Drybrushing tall grass

Although the various static grasses are realistic in height and texture,

they're too uniform in color for my taste. To simulate the colors of real tall grass, I used a variety of earth-toned acrylic paints, **7-21**. I started with Polly Scale Dirt to suggest the high-water line where the grass meets the ditch. Working up from the ditch, I then applied Weyerhauser Green and Reading Green. I drybrushed Model Master Deck Tan, Model Master Deck Umber, and Polly Scale Oxide Red along the edge of the road and railroad right-of-way.

## Finishing touches

The final step of this project was to fill the ditches with water. I started by pouring three coats of Woodland Scenics Realistic Water, **7-22**. According to the manufacturer's instructions, I poured the material in ⅛" layers, letting each application dry for 24 hours.

To alter the glass-smooth finish of the Realistic Water, I applied the firm's Water Effects using a ½" paintbrush, **7-23**. This material comes out of the bottle white but dries clear. To suggest small ripples, I stippled on a thin layer of the material. Once dry, the ditch water looked far more realistic.

# Planting other crops

If your layout is set in farm country, crop fields are a must. After all, your elevator needs commodities to load into those hoppers and boxcars.

Keeping prototype photos nearby eliminates guesswork with scenery. You can see where grass and weeds grow, where fences should be installed, and how rural grade crossings look.

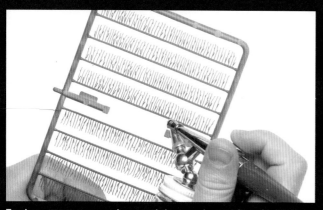

To show summer crops, I sprayed the tan wheat strips with Polly Scale Reading Green.

Trying to save time by attaching wheat strips to styrene sheet to plant crops in larger sections was not a good idea.

Having different kinds of crops adds variety to a layout. Modeling a field that looks larger than a garden requires space—and a lot of it. That's why I modeled portions of two fields. I placed a wheat field and a soybean field at the edge of the layout to suggest that the crops continue into the aisle. However, adding a field to your layout is more than just sticking plastic wheat strips or a self-adhesive mat to your scenery base. Farm grade crossings, tall grass between the field's edge and the railroad right-of-way, and shelter belts can enhance the realism of your scene.

Taking a cue from *Model Railroader* associate editor Kent Johnson, I taped prototype photos of farm fields located next to a railroad on the backdrop for reference. There are several resources for railroad photos on the Internet, but the two I used were www.railpictures.net and www.rrpicturearchives.net.

## The crops

Busch wheat field strips (no. 1204) are molded in tan plastic. Although that's a realistic color for harvest season, I wanted the wheat to look green as it would in early summer.

Since I wasn't concerned about even paint coverage, I didn't apply a primer coat to the strips. Instead, I sprayed them with Polly Scale Reading Green. After the Reading Green dried, I sprayed the top ⅛" (the head) of the strips Weyerhauser Green and the base with Polly Scale Dirt.

The wheat strips have delicate detail that can easily be damaged, so don't twist them from the sprue. Instead, use a pair of sprue cutters or spure-cutting tweezers to remove the strips from the plastic carrier.

To try and save time, I attached some wheat strips to Evergreen .020" black styrene sheet with Plastruct Bondene. To speed up the gluing process, I put

the Bondene in an A-West stainless needlepoint applicator bottle, which is quicker than applying the glue with the supplied brush. But after letting the strips dry, I ran into problems. The styrene beneath the wheat strips had curled. I tried heating the styrene under warm water to straighten it, but that didn't work (and removed some paint as well). I couldn't apply pressure from the top either, or I'd crush the wheat. I had no choice but to toss the wheat.

I ended up planting the strips of wheat one by one, securing the strips to the layout with latex adhesive caulk. If you use latex adhesive caulk, pick a color that matches your scenery base. I used tan, but brown would also work. Avoid white or other bright colors that will show up from under the scenery.

I didn't have enough wheat left to suggest a large field, so I added a soybean

I used a tweezers to plant the wheat strips one at a time.

Faller self-adhesive Germinating Seeds scenery mats can be used to represent growing soybeans.

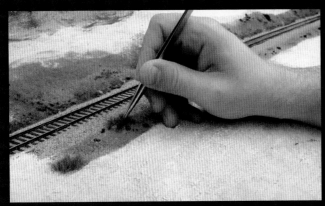
Patches of Busch Late Summer Grass provide contrast to the shorter static grass.

Trees planted between crop fields can suggest a windbreak.

field. No. 180471 self-adhesive scenery mats from Faller, Germinating Seeds, bear a resemblance to soybeans (sort of). I cut the mat to fit and attached it to the layout with full-strength white glue. These mats conform well to contours, so they work great for hilly scenes.

## Transition area
The area between the railroad right-of-way and a farm field is typically scrub land with weeds and tall grass. To re-create this, I added the scenery in layers.

First, I applied an 80/20 mixture of white glue and water along the edge of the ballast with a ½" paintbrush. With the diluted glue still wet, I sprinkled on Woodland Scenics Burnt Grass, Earth Blend, and Soil turf using a spoon. Then I sprayed the area with 70 percent isopropyl alcohol, let it soak in, and applied Woodland Scenics Scenic Cement with a pipette. While the Scenic Cement was still wet, I used a Noch Gras-Master to apply Woodland Scenics medium green static flock. The fibers are about shin high on an HO scale figure, which suggests tall grass along the right-of-way without making it look overgrown.

To provide contrast to the shorter Woodland Scenics static flock, I planted random patches of Busch no. 1304 Late Summer Grass. The grass comes on an 8¼" x 11¹¹⁄₁₆" sheet and has an adhesive backing. I tore off tufts with a pair of tweezers, dipped the tufts in full-strength white glue, and pressed them into the ground foam. I set patches of burnt grass at the edge of the ballast to suggest a weed-sprayer train has applied herbicides in this area.

As the prototype photos suggest, the railroad right-of-way isn't pretty. The grass and weeds are a mixture of light and dark green, yellow, and burnt grass. In addition, there is usually some scrub and rugged undergrowth mixed in with the tall grass. To capture that look in this scene, I applied Yellow Grass and medium and dark green coarse turf. If the turf doesn't settle between the static grass fibers, use a toothpick to press the clumps into place.

## Shelter belts
Shelter belts, or windbreaks, are commonly planted along the perimeter of fields to prevent wind damage and soil erosion. I put three Scenic Express Ready-Made trees between the wheat and soybean fields to suggest a larger shelter belt. Then I added some deadfall and clump foliage on the shelter belt floor.

*(This sidebar is condensed from an article that appeared in* Model Railroader *October 2009.)*

**8-1**

CHAPTER EIGHT    by Lance Mindheim

# Great grass, bushes, and weeds

Grassy fields with weeds, low-lying scrub, bushes, and short trees are common scenic features found along a typical right-of-way.

Grass, weeds, bushes, and short trees are some of the most important scenery elements to master because they occur with such regularity and in such great abundance across every modeling theme, **8-1**. Although seen every day, they rarely get a second glance, but if you look closely at them, they are very complex items. Colors, textures, and patterns are interwoven into something much more intricate than what can be modeled by sprinkling a bit of ground foam here and there, **8-2**. Fortunately, there has been a boom of new, high-quality scenery products to help us out.

Let's examine the main elements— grass, bushes, weeds, and short trees— and take a look at ways to combine them in a convincing fashion. None of the techniques are difficult. However, as you pull your scene together, you will have to make a conscious effort to continuously remind yourself to avoid uniform patterns and colors. Easier said than done! I also highly suggest using some form of extruded foam as your scenery base as this allows you to insert vegetation cleanly and easily.

## Modeling grass

Almost every type of layout scene is going to require grass in one form or another. In many cases, the surface area of a grassy expanse is quite large, so it is important to find ways to model it effectively. Most of the battle is won in material selection. A material that is long and fibrous is the most effec- tive in representing blades of grass. For many years, ground foam was the primary material for modeling grass. It wasn't ideal because of its more rounded shape, but it was about all that was available. In recent years, a number of fiber-based products have come on the market. When modeling grass, you want to have a product that is more fibrous in shape, and you also

8-2

A short break in the weedy scrub of Florida provides a brief glimpse of this transfer run. The variety of scenery shows a complex blend of colors, textures, and patterns.

want to avoid uniform colors, textures, and heights. Two excellent products for representing grass are static grass and grass fiber mats such as those make by Heki, **8-3**. These two products can also be comingled for variety.

Static grass is a fibrous material that, when charged with static electricity, stands on end. This property creates a very convincing representation of actual grass. The material comes in three lengths—2mm, 4mm, and 6mm—as

well as a variety of colors. The avail- ability of different shades of green is important since even within the green color palette you are going to have to mix different shades and lengths to avoid the golf-course look.

To apply static grass, you will need the static grass, a static grass applicator (for imparting a static charge to the grass as you sprinkle it on), and adhe- sives to hold the grass in place. The most effective static grass applicator

8-3

The best representation of grass blades is achieved by using fiber- based products such as static grass and fiber grass mats.

8-4

The easiest means of applying static grass is with a dedicated appli- cator such as the Noch Gras-Master. To fill in, you will need to make several passes. Apply a coating of a hair spray before each pass.

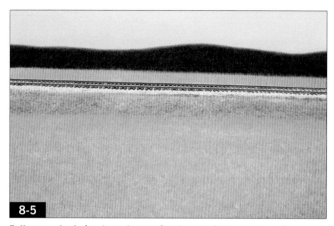

**8-5**

Follow up the beige base layer with 4mm or 6mm green static grass. Notice how the initial beige base shows through. The expanse shown here is still a bit too uniform.

**8-6**

Using grass fiber mats, such as those made by Heki, is another effective way of representing grass. The mats can be used as a stand-alone product or applied on top of static grass.

tool is an electrically charged shaker bottle called the Gras-Master, which is manufactured by Noch, **8-4**. If you don't want to invest in a Gras-Master, acceptable results can be achieved by using an ordinary spice canister and a foam block that you manually charge with static electricity.

Applying static grass with the Gras-Master is straightforward and goes quickly. Begin by spreading a thin layer of white glue over your scenery surface. I always start with an initial layer of 2mm beige grass. Heki Prairie Grass (no. 3363) works particularly well for this initial beige base. The short initial layer gives some bite for subsequent layers to adhere to. The beige base layer also ensures that your subsequent green follow-up layers won't be too uniform in color. Give your glue layer a light misting of water with a spray bottle, plug the Gras-Master probe into your scenery base, and sprinkle on the 2mm beige grass. Follow each pass with a pump of hair spray. The initial layer may not stand up vertically, but once you get the initial base down, the following layers start standing up.

Once your surface area is covered with the 2mm beige base layer, empty your Gras-Master canister and refill it with 4mm or 6mm green static grass, **8-5**. Give the surface area another spritz of hair spray and sprinkle on the green. Use caution though. With the base layer in place, the green secondary layers build up very quickly so don't overdo it. Once all of your grass is in place, seal it by applying a mix of one

part matte medium to four parts water over the grass.

The manual process is more time consuming, and not all of the fibers stand up as stiffly as when using the Noch machine. If you go the manual route, you will need to charge the grass by another means. To do this, take a 4" square of Styrofoam and rub it briskly across a sweater or your forearm until it is charged with static electricity. Shake the static grass onto the layout (covered first with a thin layer of white glue) and hold the foam block a few inches above the grass to pop it up. Spray the static grass with hairspray and repeat the process every few seconds. Again, this manual method is slow, but it does work.

You now have a grass field with realistic-looking blades, but the color is still probably too uniform and should be broken up. Take a spray can of flat green paint, such as Hunt Club Green, and add a few puffs of green here and there. Do not overspray all of the grass with the spray paint. You just want to give some subtle color variations here and there. Next, overspray a few patches of grass with hairspray, take the tiniest of pinches of ground foam, and drop a few sprinkles here and there. You are trying to minimize the use of ground foam so use a light touch.

Static grass is the fastest and easiest way to cover large expanses economically. Another product to come on the market recently is fiber grass mats, **8-6**. These are small rolls of gauze with the grass fibers already embedded in

them. The mats are very realistic on a stand-alone basis, but they can also be applied over static grass. When selecting grass fiber mats, look for products that have some subtle color and texture variations on each mat. After removing a mat from the box, grab each end with your hand and gently tear off a patch several inches square. Instead of cutting the mats with a scissors, tearing gives you a more realistic, ragged edge. After removing a patch from the roll, stretch it out a bit more. Turn it over, give it a puff of spray adhesive such as 3M Super 77, and pat it into place on the layout. Even the better-quality mats are a bit too uniform in color. To break this color up a little, finish the mats by giving the tips of the grass blades a light dry-brushing of brown, **8-7**.

## Introducing weeds

With the grass base down, the next step in the detail process is to introduce some weeds. For adding weeds, start with a bag of ordinary green poly fiber such as Woodland Scenics FP178. Take a roll of fiber and tear off part of a small clump no longer than a ½" long. Grab the clump with a pair of pointed-tip tweezers and then snip off any errant strands with a scissors. Take the tweezers and insert the clump into the foam scenery base, **8-8**. Strive for random patterns and keep the clumps small. When viewed from above, these weeds should be no larger than the tip of an pencil eraser.

Another excellent product for representing weeds is Silflor Prarie Tufts available from Scenic Express. These

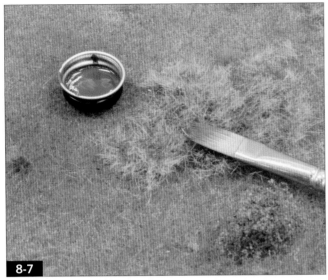

**8-7** By dry-brushing the tips of the grass blades with dark brown paint, you can break up the uniform color of the fiber grass mats.

**8-8** Small clumps of green poly-fiber weeds can quickly and easily be added to a foam scenery base with tweezers.

tufts are designed to be glued on a flat soil surface. To apply them over a completed grass field, you will need to insert them into the foam with tweezers just as you would with poly fiber.

## Adding underbrush

To help increase the sense of realism, you can break up uniform expanses of grass, ease the transition from scenery to backdrop, and mute the point where less-than-perfect tree trunks meet the ground. Often, simply making a reasonable representation of underbrush and weeds is enough to accomplish these tasks. Poly fiber is one material that you can use for bushes, shrubs, and underbrush. The keys to working with poly fiber are stretching it out into less-dense, airy pieces, adding just enough texture to give it a sense of mass, and making sure you don't have any long, errant distracting strands of fiber.

To work, take a bundle of Woodland Scenics green poly fiber and pinch off a clump about the size of a silver dollar. Make sure there are no knots or clumps. Gently pull the clump until it is about twice the size and has a very airy look to it, **8-9**. Also, make sure there are no long errant strands protruding from your patch. If there are, trim them off with a scissors. Lay the clump flat on a piece of newspaper and spray it with maximum-strength hairspray from a pump bottle. From a height of about 18", gently sprinkle on

the lightest trace of Woodland Scenics blended turf ground foam (no. T1349), **8-10**. You should only have a few sprinkles on the poly fiber. After doing a light sprinkle of foam, give it another pump with the hair spray and let it dry. Pieces about 1" to 2" long work best. If you have larger pieces simply cut them to that size with a sharp scissors. Use tweezers to gently place them on the layout as stand-alone bushes or around the bases of trees, **8-11**. It is not necessary to glue them in place since the fibers tend to snag and lock on the surrounding scenery without adhesive.

## Working with SuperTrees

The final step in the process is adding trees. Shorter scale 5- to 20-foot trees are most likely to be found along a right-of-way or in an open field.

At present, for economically modeling deciduous trees, SuperTrees from Scenic Express offer the most realistic looking armatures, **8-12**. As good as this product is, there are some methods and tips that will aid you in obtaining the best appearance. Since trees grow vertically it is important that you start with an armature that is straight. As packaged, many of the Super-Trees armatures are curved or oddly shaped. While there are techniques for straightening these armatures, this task can be very time consuming. I prefer to simply select the best pieces and discard the rest, **8-13**. The SuperTrees

plants also have small curved buds near the trunk that distract from their realism. If your tree is going to be in the foreground, you will want to remove these small buds with tweezers.

After your armatures have been cleaned and pruned, **8-14**, plant them in slab of scrap Styrofoam in preparation for painting. When viewed from a distance, most tree bark takes on a brownish, dark medium-gray cast. The color may appear different when viewed up close, but as a modeler, you want to strive to match the color seen from a distance. I've used a light gray primer to paint the armatures for leafless winter trees. However, for summer trees, I've found that light gray shows through the leaf material in a very distracting fashion. For summer trees, a better look is achieved by painting the armatures a darker gray using automobile primer, which doesn't show through as much.

After painting the armature dark gray, the last step is adding the foliage. For this, I use ground foam, but I avoid solid-green color mixes. When light hits the surface of a tree, it bounces back in a variety of green hues. To capture this look for leaves, I use a blend of green ground foam such as Woodland Scenics Green Blended Turf (no. T1349). To apply the foam to the armature, hold the tree trunk between your fingers in such a way to mask off as much of the trunk as possible. Spray the armature

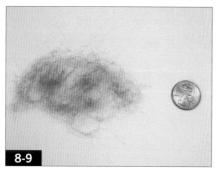

**8-9**

Start by taking a small clump of poly fiber and gently pull it apart until it is very thin and airy.

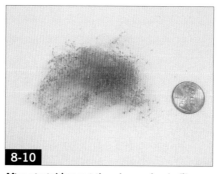

**8-10**

After stretching out the clump of poly fiber, spray it with hair spray and give it a very light dusting of ground foam.

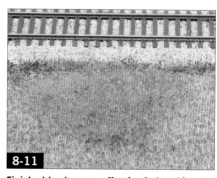

**8-11**

Finished bushes are effective in breaking up grass expanses as well as filling in below a tree's base.

**8-12**

Covering SuperTrees products with foliage is the easiest way to realistically and economically produce a group of trees.

**8-13**

The SuperTrees armatures can be clipped and combined into a variety of shapes for representing shorter trees and bushes. These armatures are ready to be painted a dark-gray color.

**8-14**

The tree on the left has been cleaned up and pruned. Notice that an armature with a nearly vertical trunk structure was selected. The finished tree on the right was coated with a light dusting of a green blend of ground foam.

with maximum-strength hair spray. Then lightly sprinkle the foam on the armature as you twirl it between your fingers. Work lightly so you do not get globs of foam. Repeat the process until the tree is covered with foam, but keep the foam off the trunk.

I generally use extruded foam as my scenery base, so planting the tree is simply a matter of punching a hole in the foam and inserting the tree, **8-15**. When placing your trees on the layout, it is very important to keep them as vertical as possible. It is also important when placing trees on the layout that you clump them in random groups and patterns. Mix up the height and spac-ing of the trees to avoid the appearance of a manicured garden.

For very small trees and bushes, there are two ways to use SuperTrees prod-ucts. One is to simply snip a short 1" section of the armature and paint and texture it as described for trees. Another method is to snip off a number of indi-vidual branches, clump them together, and then paint and texture them.

So there you have it. We start with a grass layer made from fibrous materials, insert some weeds, add bushes to break up transitions, and finish by planting trees. The key is to keep all of the patterns as random as they are found in nature.

**8-15**

After inserting the tree into the scenery, conceal the point where the trunk meets the ground by working in a poly-fiber bush around the base.

CHAPTER NINE    by Lance Mindheim

# Dry, detailed creekbeds

As the dog days of summer wear on with limited rainfall, creeks that handle less water volume begin to contract and, in some cases, may dry up completely. Because dry creeks and streams are fairly common in nature, it makes sense to incorporate a few here and there on a model railroad. They provide an interesting modeling subject because the absence of water allows you to see the exposed creekbed and all of its details, **9-1**. Dry streams are also a bit easier to build because you don't have to model the water. The process of building a dry stream is identical to that of modeling a traditional water-filled creek—except you skip the last step of adding water. But because the creek bottom is exposed, you will want to put more time into detailing it.

**In a dry creekbed, you will see a collection of branches, rocks, and debris. Note the pump house foundation at the edge of the creek. The creek has been dry long enough for weeds to have sprouted up.**

## Laying out and cutting the creekbed

The process of modeling a dry stream starts with forming the stream channel. Extruded foam as a scenery base provides the most flexibility because it is inexpensive and easy to carve, cut, and shape. The first steps are cutting the route of the stream channel and forming the stream bottom. One option is simply carving out a basin with a hot-wire foam cutter. While this method will work, it can be time consuming and also difficult in maintaining a uniform depth. I've found it is easier to form stream channels if you place a slab of ¾" foam for the stream channel on top of your overall foam scenery base, 9-2.

Mark your stream route with a pen on the ¾" slab of foam, 9-3. Then add gentle meanders and curve the stream to one side or the other as it approaches the backdrop, 9-4. With a dry creek, a variety of widths, down to something extremely narrow, is appropriate. Since the detailed stream bottom is going to be exposed, though, you might consider modeling a wider stream, perhaps something in the 4" to 5" range.

After laying out the stream route, cut out the stream channel at your

workbench with a utility knife, 9-5. When done, temporarily lay the ¾" foam in position on your scenery base (don't glue it down), mark the stream channel route on the base foam, and remove the top foam piece, 9-6.

Next, gently sand slopes and undercuts into the channel sides of the upper foam piece, 9-7. In many cases, the terrain in the immediate vicinity of the creek will be relatively flat. Even so, you will want to introduce some subtle undulations. Using coarse sandpaper, a hot wire foam cutter, or a power sander, gently work some shallow dips and

depressions into the foam around the creek, 9-8. Be sure to wear a dust mask when doing this.

Now that the creek banks and the areas around the creek have been formed, let's turn our attention to the creek bottom. A shallow bowl in the scenery base is all that is needed. Use sandpaper or a sander to work a shallow depression (⅛" to ¼") into the scenery base to represent the stream bottom, 9-9. Then, after completing the creek bottom, position the top foam piece over the scenery base and glue it in place with hot glue.

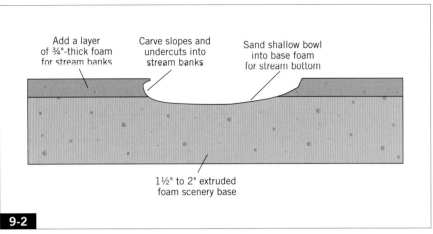

**9-2**

Rather than carving the entire stream from a single block of foam, it is easier to sandwich two layers of foam on top of one another.

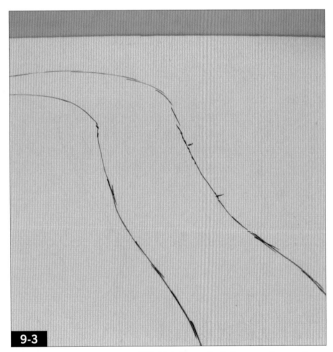

**9-3**

Sketch your stream route on ¾"-thick foam. Include meanders and curve the stream out of view as it approaches the backdrop. This foam piece will be added to the layout after the stream banks are sanded.

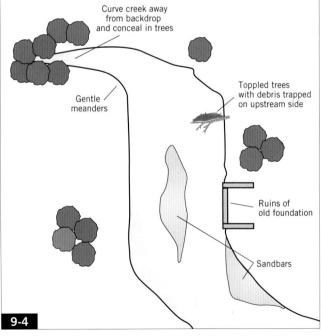

**9-4**

This top view of the creekbed shows the position of several sandbars and how the creek narrows as it approaches the backdrop.

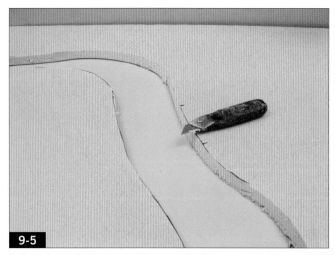

**9-5**

Before gluing the top layer of foam to the base, cut out the stream with a utility knife.

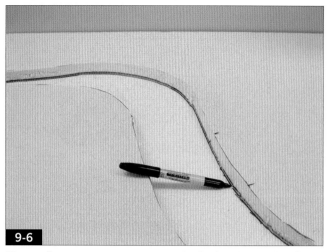

**9-6**

After cutting out your stream route on the top foam layer, place it over the base and mark the stream route out on the foam base.

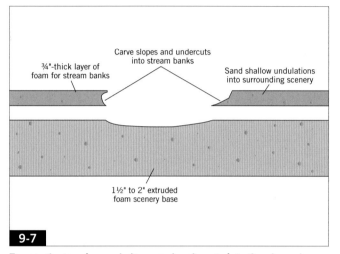

¾"-thick layer of foam for stream banks

Carve slopes and undercuts into stream banks

Sand shallow undulations into surrounding scenery

1 ½" to 2" extruded foam scenery base

**9-7**

To vary the terrain, sand slopes and undercuts into the channel sides and add some undulations to the surrounding flat terrain around the creek.

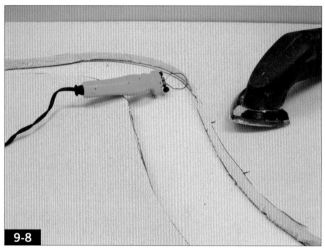

**9-8**

Use a hot wire foam cutter or a sander to shape gentle scenery contours and work undercuts and slopes into the stream banks.

## Preparing the scenery base

With the stream channel roughed in, the next step is to prepare the foam for the next level of textures. In order to hide cracks, seams, and imperfections in the foam, give the entire scenery base a very thin coat of ordinary drywall joint compound, **9-10**. Simply spread it over the base with your hand, making sure to cover any obvious irregularities or gaps in the foam. Follow up with a paintbrush dipped in water and brush the joint compound layer smooth.

When the joint compound is dry, or nearly dry, paint the entire surface a neutral earth tone, **9-11**. For coloring the scenery base, I prefer inexpensive acrylic craft paint, which is available at craft stores. Simply, pick a few shades

of tan and brown, squirt the paint on your scenery surface, and swish it around with a wet paintbrush until everything is coated.

## Forming muddy creek banks

Since the creek banks are vertical or steeply sloped, traditional methods of sprinkling on dry scenery soils to texture the banks won't work. You need something with more adhesion. Take some earth scenery material of your choice and pour it in a shallow cup. Slowly stir in diluted white glue until you've created a mix that has the consistency of, well, mud or a milk shake, **9-12**. Take a worn-out brush and paint the mud onto your stream banks and let it dry. Make sure you work it under the lip of your undercut.

## Placing a foundation

To add a little interest, I decided to add the ruins of an old structure foundation along the stream bank, **9-13**. This could represent the foundation of long-since abandoned mill or a pump house. A trip to the scrap box uncovered a few pieces of old abutments and piers from Chooch Enterprises. Without being scientific about it, I picked out a few sections that were four- or five-stone courses high. I arranged them into a roughly rectangular shape and glued them together with superglue. I used Squadron putty to fill in the seams. When the glue and putty dried, I brushed on a layer of Polly Scale L&N Gray. When the base gray had dried, I applied a thin wash of diluted India ink to bring out the stone detail. You could

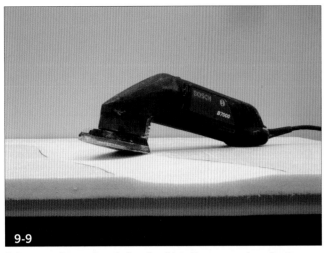

9-9

Using a sander, work a shallow bowl into the scenery base for the stream bottom. When you've contoured the top foam layer and shaped the stream bottom into your scenery base, hot-glue the layers together.

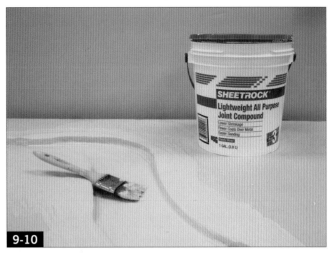

9-10

After the top foam layer has been glued to the base, seal everything by brushing on a thin layer of joint compound.

9-11

When you've sealed your scenery base with joint compound and it has dried, paint the base with neutral, earth-toned acrylic craft paint.

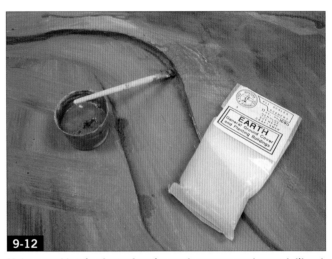

9-12

Make a muddy mix of your favorite earth scenery product and diluted white glue and paint it on the stream banks.

also use a thin wash of dark gray acrylic paint to get the same result. When the foundation was completed, I cut a notch in the stream bank with a utility knife and set the foundation in place.

## Detailing the creek bottom

After the mud on your stream banks has dried, you can begin detailing the bottom. I've found that this is easier if you do it in several layers, allowing each layer to dry before adding another. Any mix of gray aggregates will do, **9-14**. Strive for using a variety of textures but try to avoid larger, rounder, pebbles. Also vary the shades of gray for the best look. Some of the best sources of streambeds come from track ballast suppliers. Salt-and-pepper blends of ballast (N scale looks best),

asphalts, and dark grays are all good. Arizona Rock and Mineral Company even makes a dedicated product called Stream Bottom, although it has a lot of larger pebbles in it that should be strained out first.

A good starting point would be to put down a layer of ordinary, N scale, salt-and-pepper colored track ballast, **9-15**. Spray it with water mixed with a splash of alcohol. Next, slowly drip on an adhesive (a mix of one part white glue and four parts water) just as you would to track ballast and let it dry. Follow that layer with darker ballast down the middle of the stream and glue it down. Finally, sprinkle a light layer of tiny, ground-up plaster chips down the center of the stream and glue those in place. As you detail the

bottom, be sure to add sandbars here and there. Visualize how the stream flows when it is filled and where the water would deposit debris and create sandbars.

## Adding vegetation

After you are satisfied with the placement of the soils and aggregate on your streambed, direct your attention to adding some vegetation. If the streambed has been water-free for some time, it's likely that a few weeds will be poking up. Give the bed a few puffs of hairspray and then put a tiny pinch of green ground foam between you fingers and sprinkle a bit here and there. Keep the sprinkled-on ground foam very light and sparse. After the foam sprinkles are in place, give them

**9-13**

The ruins of an old foundation were fabricated out of scrap pieces from another project.

**9-14**

Detail the stream bottom with various shades of gray ballast and soils. N scale ballast, with its finer blend is ideal. Run coarser mixes through a strainer to remove the large pebbles.

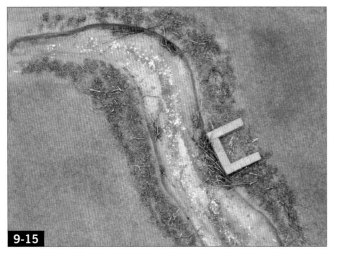

**9-15**

This overhead view of the dry streambed shows the effects that can be obtained by layering several tones and textures of soil and ballast. Note the plaster chips along the center of the stream.

**9-16**

The streambed includes fallen tree limbs and accumulated natural debris. The surrounding area also includes fallen tree branches, which are best represented by real twigs.

one more puff of hair spray to seal them in position. Additional weeds can be modeled with Silfor Prairie Tufts. These tufts come in a variety of sizes, but for the streambed, the best look is obtained by using the smallest or shortest Prairie Tufts.

When the stream is carrying water, it would likely undercut its banks, eventually causing the trees closest to the bank to lean over and eventually topple into the water. There should be at least a few dead or rotting tree trunks and other limb debris in your streambed, **9-16**. For the most natural appearance, look outside for real twigs. Be sure to use twigs that scale down and don't have odd shapes or branches splitting off at unrealistic sharp angles.

Azalea limbs and tumbleweeds are two good sources of dead trunk material.

When water flows in a stream, it will sweep leaves and smaller limbs downstream until they are trapped on the upstream side of toppled trunks. To add leaf debris, go to the backyard, pick up some leaves, grind them between your fingers or through a sifter, and sprinkle them on the upstream side of fallen trunks.

## Surrounding scenery

After the creek bottom details are complete, bring the rest of your layout's scenery up to the stream and feather it in. Start by sprinkling some dead limb debris around the area bordering the creek and then

do the bushes and other vegetation. Although the creek is dry, the surrounding environment has, or will have had, enough moisture to produce thicker surrounding vegetation. The trees and bushes around the creekbed should be thicker than the rest of the surrounding area. Trees may even arch completely over the bed, creating the effect of being in a tunnel.

## Choosing water options

Creekbeds see the full spectrum of water volume and aren't just completely wet or dry. One interesting option might be to have a few pools of standing water in the low spots. Another option might be to have a small ribbon of water running down the dry creekbed.

10-1

Photos by the author

CHAPTER TEN    by Gerry Leone

# Lily pads, cattails, and pond scum

Near a railroad right-of-way, a pair of ducks swim in a pond detailed with lily pads, cattails, pond scum, grasses, and fallen branches.

Even if you're not modeling my home state, the Land of 10,000 Lakes, your layout may have a lowlands area that could use a small lake, pond, or bog. These shallow, quiet bodies of fresh water usually contain cattails, lily pads, and pond scum, **10-1**. Here are a few simple techniques for modeling those details.

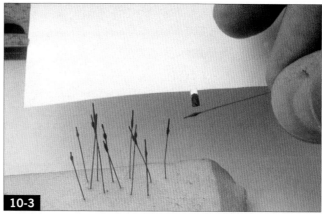

10-2

In summertime, with their green stalks, cattails blend in with tall grasses. The perennial herbs can reach a height of 5 feet or more.

10-3

To model the Plastruct rod stalk, cut a small tab in a piece of paper and put nail polish on the tab. A thick book holds the tab in place as you paint the stalk.

## Two shakes of a cat's tail

Cattails are common perennial herbs that grow anywhere from 5 to 9 feet high, **10-2**. Modeling cattails takes several steps, but the process lends itself to making dozens at a time.

For HO scale, use Plastruct .010" plastic rod cut into approximately 1" lengths for the main stalks. To color the rods, hold them with tweezers and dunk each into a bottle of Polly Scale Coach Green, a color that blends in nicely with Woodland Scenics ground foam colors. Then let the stalks dry thoroughly.

Cut a small tab, about 6 scale inches across, from a piece of heavy paper. This will be your paintbrush for creating the cattail's velvety brown seed pod. Put the paper between the pages of a book to hold the tab above your workbench and then place a sizable drop of brown nail polish on the end of the tab, **10-3**.

Wait a minute or so for the nail polish to thicken. Hold the Plastruct rod parallel with the paper-painting tab and drag about 6 scale inches of the tip through the polish, creating a blob. As you drag, roll the rod between your fingers to distribute the polish evenly. Poke the rod into a small scrap of rigid foam to dry.

Be careful not to use too much nail polish—not only will the cattail be oversized, but the enamel in the nail polish will weaken the plastic. For fat cattails, it's better to use two thinner coats and let the polish dry in between. If your blob is too bulbous or poorly

shaped, let it dry for a minute or two and then reshape it by gently rolling it on the surface of your workbench or between your fingers.

Once the polish hardens, dip the top of the cattail into Polly Scale Roof Brown. The final step is to paint the top 6" spike of the cattail, again by tweezer-dunking. The color on this end varies: in midsummer, it's a vibrant rust orange (Polly Scale Rust), but as fall nears, the color changes to beige (Polly Scale Concrete).

## Green and gold grasses

I use Envirotex Lite two-part epoxy to model water. It's easy to work with, and its surface dries completely level, which is perfect for small, still bodies of water such as woodland ponds. It's easier to plant most of the grasses before pouring the resin.

Your shoreline and shallow water should contain an abundance of the tall grasses that cattails grow in. I mix Woodland Scenics medium green, dark green, and gold tall grasses to show new, mature, and dead vegetation respectively. Use white glue to cement pencil-diameter-sized bundles to the shore as well as several scale feet out onto the water surface. It's best to space the initial plantings widely apart. Once the glue dries, you can plant more, getting the vegetation as dense and even as possible.

Once the Envirotex has set, go back and use white glue to attach a small amount of additional grass in front of the grass you previously

planted. This hides any areas where the Envirotex may have crept up the stems of the grass bunches. Cut your cattails slightly shorter than the tallest grass, and use a drop of cyanoacrylate adhesive or white glue to plant them among the grasses.

## Lily pads with a punch

Lily pads, the leaves of water lily plants, flourish along the shallow shorelines and quiet inlets of larger bodies of fresh water, **10-4**. The 6" to 15" broad leaves are medium green when young, dark green when mature, yellow while dying, and brown once dead. Many leaves contain several colors. Lily pads usually grow in great abundance, with the leaves often overlapping one another as the plants fight for sunlight.

The easiest way to model lily pads is to punch them out— literally — by the dozen, **10-5**. First, put several drops of Polly Scale Reefer Yellow, Coach Green, and Roof Brown on a piece of white paper. Use a paintbrush to mix, overpaint, and push the colors around the paper at random. Then let the paint dry completely.

To make the lily pad punches, chose several short lengths of brass tubing with inner diameters ranging from 1/16" to 1/8". Use an awl or nail set to flare the end of each tube slightly and chuck it into a variable-speed electric drill. Run the drill at slow speed while holding a round needle file in the open end of the tube. In a minute or two, you'll have a sharp cutting edge.

**10-4**

Water lily plants grow in great multicolored clusters in larger bodies of fresh water. Note the notches in the leaves where the stems are.

**10-5**

Paint a piece of paper with a variety of colors and use a sharpened piece of brass tubing to punch out lily pads by the dozen.

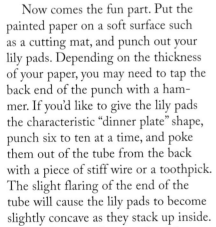

**10-6**

By late summer, algae and duckweed can completely cover the surface of a small body of water.

**10-7**

When adding scum to a small body of water, modeling it as shown in photo 10-6 would be overkill and overwhelm your other details.

Now comes the fun part. Put the painted paper on a soft surface such as a cutting mat, and punch out your lily pads. Depending on the thickness of your paper, you may need to tap the back end of the punch with a hammer. If you'd like to give the lily pads the characteristic "dinner plate" shape, punch six to ten at a time, and poke them out of the tube from the back with a piece of stiff wire or a toothpick. The slight flaring of the end of the tube will cause the lily pads to become slightly concave as they stack up inside.

Cut the stem slot in each of the lily pads with a sharp hobby knife and glue the lily pads to the surface of your pond, making sure to randomly overlap their edges.

## Pond scum

In summer, the combination of heat, humidity, and sunlight is perfect for the development of scum on small bodies of water, **10-6** and **10-7**. This green scum actually comes from one of two biological sources: algae and duckweed. It's most prevalent on smaller ponds, although it does accumulate on the windward shores of larger bodies of water.

To simulate scum if your pond is already in place, sprinkle fine ground foam (Woodland Scenics Weeds or Grass works well) along the shoreline and use diluted white glue or matte medium to secure the ground foam to your Envirotex water.

If you have yet to pour your pond, try this. After the Envirotex has set for about 45 minutes, use a toothpick to dab small droplets of Floquil Coach Green directly onto the surface, right next to the shore. Over the next hour, the paint will spread an inch or so, turning from solid green into

a network of extremely fine green flecks. The result is a convincing scum that's part of the surface and can't be damaged.

When choosing your scum color, be sure to compensate for any tinting you have added to your Envirotex as this will affect the final color. If you space your initial paint dabs far enough apart, surface tension and drying will keep them from mixing together. This forms convincing "critter trails" to the shore.

Dressing up a small lake, pond, or bog can be an interesting modeling diversion. Some would even call it a quiet refuge (pun intended) from the daily demands of a layout!

A special thanks to Dr. Dick Osgood, good friend and limnologist, for some of the technical details in this article.

*(First appeared in* Model Railroader *March 2001)*

11-1

Photos by the author

CHAPTER ELEVEN    by Lance Mindheim

# Abandoned rails and trails

Over the centuries, the American rail network has constantly evolved, going through periods of expansion and contraction. Depending on the time period you are modeling, railroads could have been laying new rail to increase capacity or abandoning lines that were no longer needed. In some cases, both may have been happening simultaneously. An abandoned railroad right-of-way is fascinating by-product to model, **11-1**. When standing on an abandoned right-of-way on a bright summer day, and looking into the distance, you can't help but imagine a more prosperous time for that particular line—a time when what is now a weedy path to nowhere once carried manifest freights and streamlined passenger trains.

Having become obsolete, a rail line that once carried manifest freights and streamlined passenger trains now serves as a scenic hiking trail. Such scenes dot the land and would be a realistic addition to almost any model railroad.

**11-2**

Abandoned track can take many forms. In this photo, what was once the Seaboard Airline double-track main into downtown Miami is now a single-track branch line, with an abandoned second track on the right.

**11-3**

The orientation of structures often provide hints to the location of past rail lines. Note the rail still embedded in the street.

**11-4**

This overhead view illustrates some common features of an abandoned right-of-way. The rails have been removed but the ties remain. Some structures have been demolished, leaving their exposed foundations. Scrap ties and tie plates lay scattered about, and the original telegraph poles still stand.

**11-5**

Before getting started, it is helpful to construct a simple mock-up to check the sight lines and scene composition.

Abandoned rights-of-way take on many forms. Some have been paved over and made into biking and hiking trails. Others have been left completely untouched with rails and ties still in place but with vegetation encroaching more and more each year. Given the value of scrap steel, a common scenario is having the rails removed and sold for scrap. When rails are removed for scrap, sometimes the ties are left in place and, in some instances, the ties are removed with the rail. There are also cases of partial abandonment, such as a double-track line that has been downsized to a single track, **11-2**. Other interesting features of abandoned lines are the surrounding rail structures, **11-3**. At the site of an old interlocking tower, the foundation and a few small sheds might remain. Concrete bridge abutments and piers often stand for decades (or centuries) after the rail and bridge have been scrapped. Rails often remain in the pavement at grade crossings as well. When it comes to modeling an abandoned rail scene, you are limited only by your imagination.

Let's take a look at modeling a rail crossing where one of the main lines has been abandoned while the other is still in service, **11-4**. This example suggests busier days when the crossing was served by an interlocking tower and its associated service sheds. Let's assume the rails have been removed for scrap but the ties are still in place. The right-of-way has started to fill in with weeds, but it isn't so choked off with vegetation that the line is obscured. Some structures have been demolished, leaving their foundations exposed. Perhaps a dilapidated shed or two still stands as do the original telegraph poles. We will also look at how to model the way vegetation slowly envelops the abandoned line.

## Composing the scene

Before jumping right into the modeling, it is helpful to do a rough mock-up of the scene, **11-5**. Begin by setting the angle of the abandoned line as it

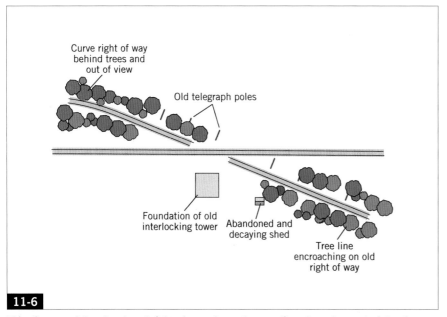

Curve right of way
behind trees and
out of view

Old telegraph poles

Foundation of old
interlocking tower

Abandoned and
decaying shed

Tree line
encroaching on old
right of way

**11-6**

This diagram of the abandoned right-of-way shows the tree line along the track right-of-way as well as telegraph poles and other features.

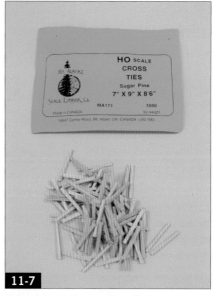

**11-7**

Natural wood ties work well when modeling abandoned track because they take stain easily.

**11-8**

Start by giving the wood ties an initial base coat of light gray using a solvent-based paint such as Model Master Light Gray.

**11-9**

After the gray base coat has dried for a day, you can create the look of faded creosote by adding a wash of oil paint.

crosses the active line. Try to avoid having your abandoned line running into the backdrop at a right angle. If the abandoned line curves out of sight as it approaches the backdrop, it gives the illusion that it continues into the distance. Also, make sure the angle is not too sharp, so you have room for the structures.

Once you are satisfied with the alignment, lay out the centerline and then the cork roadbed for the base of the abandoned line. Next, lay out the location of your structures and foundations using pieces of paper to represent them. Move the scraps around until you are satisfied with the overall orientation. With

the route of the abandoned line set, the cork laid, and the basic position of the structures set, you can start modeling the elements that make up the scene, **11-6**.

## Placing ties

Where the ties are still in place, it is likely that they will have a split, worn, and faded look to them. Natural wood ties would be good to use in this environment because they can be stained a very realistic faded appearance, **11-7**. To place the ties, lay a thin line of white glue along your cork roadbed and place the wood ties in place over the route of the abandoned track. Since you are representing a ragged affair,

don't be overly concerned about tie spacing. Leave a few ties out here and there. Stick a hobby-knife blade into a few of the ties and twist the blade to slightly split them. You can also create scrap ties for later use by breaking some ties by hand or splitting them more with a knife.

After the glue has dried, stain the ties a very faded driftwood gray, **11-8**. When staining wood, I've found that I achieve better results if I use solvent-based paint such as Model Master Light Gray (no. FS36495). After painting the ties gray, let them dry for at least a day. Once the base gray stain has dried, the next step is to add a look of faded

**11-10**

Forms for foundation slabs are quickly and easily constructed out of styrene scraps. Before pouring the cement into the mold, remember to wipe some WD-40 over the mold to serve as a release agent.

**11-11**

Mix the cement to the consistency of a milk shake, pour it into the mold, and let it cure overnight.

**11-12**

After the cement has cured, gently pry the castings out of the mold.

**11-13**

Place the castings on the layout with white glue and run your scenery up to the edges. A nice effect can be obtained by introducing cracks into the castings by pushing down on them firmly with your fingers.

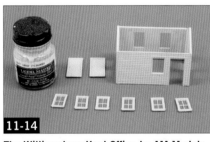

**11-14**

The Williamsburg Yard Office by AM Models is representative of service sheds found almost everywhere. After assembling the walls, I airbrushed the structure a light gray.

**11-15**

To give the effect of peeling paint, dry-brush the final color with a chisel-shaped brush. Run the brush strokes in the same direction as the siding.

creosote, **11-9**. To do this, follow up with a wash of Raw Umber (an artist oil thinned with mineral spirits). Minwax Jacobean wood stain also works well as a creosote stain. After the ties dry, apply ballast around the ties as you would along any other rail on your layout.

## Building concrete foundations

Even when a structure has been torn down (or burned down), the foundation often remains in place. The foundation may be chipped, faded, or cracked but it will still stand. I chose to use several such foundations to model several "ruins." Rather than using styrene, I wanted a material with a little more texture as well as something that would simulate the cracks that would likely appear over time. And what could be more suitable than actual cement? While actual cement is too coarse to scale down for modeling purposes, a material called anchor bolt cement fills the bill nicely. (My article "Making Concrete Bridges" in the August 2007

issue of *Model Railroader* outlines how to use anchor bolt cement castings.)

Making your own concrete castings is a simple process that essentially copies what happens in 1:1, real-life scale. Start by making a simple form out of styrene for your concrete slab, **11-10**. For slabs, there really isn't much to it. Lay a scrap piece of .060" styrene sheet on your workbench. If you want to represent expansion joints, scribe those into the form with the back of a no. 11 hobby blade. Build up the sides with .010" square styrene strip. Wipe the form with a cotton swab that has been moistened with WD-40 to add a mold release. Put a bit of the anchor bolt cement in a small paper cup and slowly add water until it has the consistency of a milk shake. Pour the mix into your form and tap the sides of the form to release any trapped air bubbles, **11-11**. Then allow the cement to dry overnight, and when it has cured, simply pry it from the mold, **11-12**. In case the casting cracks, simply glue it back

together with super-glue gel as if you were repairing a broken plate. Place the casting on the layout and glue it in place with a few dabs of white glue, **11-13**. Bring your scenery up to the edges of the casting. If the casting didn't crack when you removed it from the mold, you might want to add a few breaks to simulate a foundation slowly being broken down by the elements. After the casting is in place on the layout surface, firmly push down on casting with your finger to cause it to crack.

## Modeling small sheds

After a right-of-way has been abandoned, there is really no consistent pattern as to which structures are demolished and which ones remain standing. It is fairly common to see smaller sheds still standing many decades later. Their paint may be peeling and the windows boarded up but they still remain. To model one such structure, I chose the Williamsburg

**11-16**

Boarded-up windows were made with scraps of stripwood stained with a light India ink and alcohol wash.

**11-17**

Prairie Tufts, available from Scenic Express, make excellent lineside weeds.

**11-18**

Add a small drop of white glue to the Prairie Tufts and place them between the ties, along the right-of-way, and around the structure foundations.

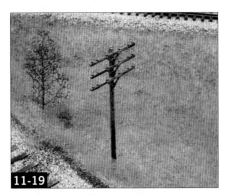

**11-19**

Telegraph poles often stand for many years after a line has been abandoned.

**11-20**

A number of vendors make etched metal tie plates. Paint or chemically blacken a few and place them on a some ties.

**11-21**

When you stain wooden ties, make some extra scraps and scatter them by the side of the right-of-way.

Yard Office kit by AM Models, **11-14**. This simple kit is very nicely cast and is also very representative of sheds found all over the country.

I built the walls and airbrushed them with Model Master Light Gray. After the base gray dried, I created the effect of peeling paint by following up with a light dry-brushing of Boxcar Red, **11-15**. I boarded up the windows with stripwood lightly stained with a diluted mix of India ink and alcohol, **11-16**.

## Handling typical vegetation

Handling the vegetation is one of the keys to convincingly model an abandoned right-of-way. When a line is in service, the railroad meticulously keeps trees trimmed back and eliminates weeds with sprayers. When the line is abandoned, this maintenance obviously stops, and Mother Nature quickly moves back in. Some examples of typical vegetation overgrowth are weeds sprouting up between the abandoned

ties and interlocking area, small 6- to 10-foot trees growing in these same areas, and previously trimmed mature trees that line the right-of-way now arching over it.

Short weeds can be created from Scenic Express Prairie Tufts, which come in 2mm, 4mm, and 6mm heights as well as a variety of colors, **11-17**. To add, simply pluck the tufts off their backing sheet, apply some white glue to the bottom, and set them in place in a random pattern, **11-18**. Place weeds between the ties and around the abandoned foundations. Have a few weeds sprout up from the foundation cracks as well.

## Completing final details

As is the case with small sheds, telegraph poles often remain in place long after a line is abandoned, **11-19**. I chose to include one such row along the right-of-way. I started out with ordinary Atlas telephone poles (no. 775) and airbrushed them with Model

Master Light Gray. After the gray had dried, I applied the same Raw Umber oil-stain wash that I used on the ties and let the stain dry for several days. I dusted the poles with brown weathering chalks and sealed everything with Dullcote. To complete, I painted the insulators with Polly Scale L&N Gray.

A look into the scrap box revealed some photoetched tie plates, **11-20**. I chemically blackened a few of these using a commercial blackening agent, put a few on the ties, and scattered about several more, **11-21**. I also took some of the leftover wooden ties, particularly the more chewed-up pieces, and scattered them parallel to the right-of-way.

Because abandoned infrastructure is such a common feature of the railroad scene, it makes a unique and realistic addition to almost any model railroad. As we've seen, such ruins can take on many forms. The next time you are out railfanning and come across one, take some photos to give you some ideas.

# Right-of-way embankment vegetation

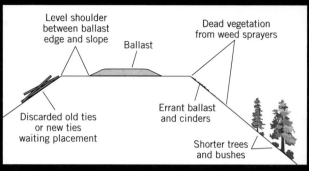

In this embankment scene, notice the brown grass near the ballast that was killed off by weed sprayers. Surrounding vegetation is relatively low, having been trimmed back from the right-of-way. Ballast and old cinders slough down the slope.

To represent the grass killed by weed spraying, apply a layer of beige static grass. Then mask the top of the embankment with a rag or towel before following up with green static grass.

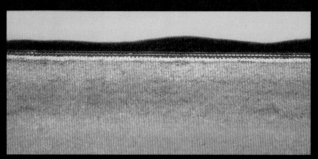

After removing the masking rag, you will have a subtle transition from dead grass at the top the embankment to darker green grass lower on the embankment.

Detail your embankment with ballast and cinders sloughing down the slope and an occasional weed. Here, the maintenance-of-way crew has also left new ties for future installation.

Finish the detailing by working small trees and brush toward the bottom of the slope.

The slopes of a railroad embankment are common places to find scrub and low-lying vegetation. To ensure adequate drainage and protection against flooding, most rail rights-of-way are built on elevated embankments. The height of an embankment will vary with conditions and surrounding topography, but even in the flattest of areas, the rails will be at least elevated slightly above the surrounding soil.

I form the embankment out of blocks of foam, cut to the appropriate slope angle and worked up to the side of the plywood roadbed. Make sure to leave at least a slight shoulder between the edge of the ballast and the point where the top of the slope starts. Embankment vegetation is often slightly different than the surrounding scenery as the railroad strives to keep all plant life from encroaching too close to the track. Weeds are kept in check by spraying, which may kill much of the vegetation several feet on each side of the ballast. Trees here also need to be trimmed back. If there are any trees found at all on an embankment, they are likely to be shorter ones. Gravity also comes into play. As the line is re-ballasted, cinders and ballast slough and tumble down the sides of the slope. Occasionally, ties will need to be replaced. After replacement, the old ties are often just thrown over the sides of the slope. New ties are commonly dropped at the top of an embankment prior to the tie crew coming by for installation.

So when modeling an embankment, place some dead and brown foliage close to the ballast, keep the surrounding vegetation short, and spill some occasional ballast and cinders down the slope.

**12-1**

Photos by the author

CHAPTER TWELVE    by Mike Danneman

# Summer backdrop tips

Many of us choose summer as the season to set our model railroad in, **12-1**. And why not? The beautiful weather of a gorgeous summer day can easily beckon us back to better times, the times that we so eagerly try to portray in our miniature world.

A detouring Union Pacific streamliner graces the rails of the Rio Grande in N scale. Summer abounds in this view. Snow on the peaks has melted except in the highest elevations, spring grasses have started to mature and brown, and the aspens shimmer in summer greens.

12-2

Summer trees are dark green, but notice the lighter, hazy background colors. An old brush is useful when stippling acrylic paint on your backdrop when painting trees. So don't throw out those worn-out brushes!

12-3

Norfolk Southern train No. 180 works through Tateville, Ky., on August 23, 1992. A hot and humid day has descended on the mountains, and the hazy conditions create a beautiful layered effect. With fewer details needed, this Eastern mountain scene is easy to paint as a backdrop.

12-4

Two Wisconsin Central SD45s power a southbound at Theresa, Wis., on July 23, 1995. The lower angle emphasizes the sky, and the clouds blend smoothly into the gorgeous summer sky.

12-5

Summer thunderstorms approach as BNSF's Beer Train to Golden, Colo., returns to Denver on August 30, 2000. Sometimes the sky on your backdrop doesn't have to include a lot of blue sky to be effective.

When finishing off a summer backdrop, keep in mind the color of the foliage and the conditions of the sky. Summer trees normally have deep, dark green leaves. When painting a summer backdrop, match the tone of these greens on your modeled trees, only lighten them on the backdrop to give the illusion of distance, **12-2**. In many parts of the country, summer brings humidity and hazy conditions, **12-3**. Lighter foliage colors on a backdrop indicate a hazy atmosphere. The same goes for the sky-blue color you use for your backdrop. Summer conditions will render the sky a much lighter blue, sometimes approaching a cool off-white color. Use the humidity in the air to your advantage by hazing the colors of your backdrop, and simplifying the detail necessary to complete the job.

Summer grasses seen on the backdrop will be less green and more brown and yellow due to hot temperatures and a possible lack of summer rain. By not using as much green as in a spring backdrop, you can present the look of a hot summer day, complete with maturing leaves on trees and bushes as well as drying crops and grasses.

Summer skies are also associated with puffy, white clouds. Fair-weather cumulous clouds are common in this season, so make sure to them to your backdrop. You can use commercial or handmade stencils to recreate these clouds on the backdrop, or you can try painting a few with artist's acrylic paints. I use titanium white and Payne's Gray acrylics mixed with the blue latex paint I use as the sky color. Using sky blue allows me to nicely blend the clouds into the sky, **12-4**.

Begin by applying some titanium white on your backdrop where you want a cloud, and begin forming the very white top of the cloud. Then use some sky blue to feather the outer edges. More white can be added at any time to increase the cloud's size or to create different shapes within each cloud. Color the underside of the cloud with a very small amount of Payne's Gray. This color can be made more subtle by adding sky blue or white. Carefully blend the colors to give the cloud a soft blend and shape.

Make sure to have clouds of different sizes and shapes, **12-5**. Smaller clouds are more likely found at the horizon, and they become larger the closer they are to the layout. Also keep the clouds in random groupings, so the sky doesn't have an evenly peppered look. Leave some sky empty for a varied look.

by David Popp

Rolling, tree-covered hills are a great subject for modeling autumn colors. My N scale New Haven layout is set in fall 1958, so the brightly colored hillsides look right at home. *Photo by David Popp*

As daylight gets shorter and shorter, nature brings out its fireworks for one last hurrah. Autumn leaves in vibrant reds, yellows, purples, oranges, and bright greens suddenly abound. Even the browns of the oak trees and the tans of the tall grasses look spectacular. Everywhere you look, there's an explosion of warm earth tones and rustic color.

I've always liked fall, but until I built my N scale Naugatuck Valley layout, I'd never modeled it. I figured that the rolling, deciduous tree-covered hills of Connecticut were as good a place as any to try modeling an autumn landscape, and so I decided early on in the design of the layout that I would set it in the fall of 1959.

When it came time to add the scenery to the first section of the layout, I bought a healthy supply of ready-made trees in autumn colors and installed them on the railroad—straight from the box. Needless to say, my first attempts at achieving convincing fall scenery were not at all satisfactory.

The main faults I find with most layouts set in fall, including my own first attempt, are that the colors used are too garish and too evenly applied. Most autumn trees in the real world don't change color all at once, and even the trees that do appear to be a solid color, such as a bright yellow maple, actually have many variations of color in their leaves when you look at them closely. The model trees I'd originally used were made in uniformly solid, bright colors, and to make realistic tree-covered hills, that had to change. I experimented with paint, various colors of ground foam, and other things to improve the look of my fall trees. You can also take another approach and model late fall when there are no leaves on the trees (Chapter Fifteen).

Another key point in modeling realistic autumn scenery is tree placement. Many times you'll find clusters, both large and small, of the same type of tree growing together in one location. There may be a few interlopers scattered about whose seeds had been dropped by some animal, and the resulting tress have managed to get a jump on their neighbors, but then another cluster of similar trees will appear.

Just like the rest of nature, trees fight over turf and attempt to crowd out those that are not their own kind. Other than what you'll find in newly built subdivisions, there is no landscaping plan for a natural hillside, so avoid planting trees in a predictable arrangement.

While you're working on building a fall scene, don't forget grasses and fields. The static-grass revolution has made modeling the tall grass of late summer and early fall easier than ever. I've been retrofitting the scenery on my layout using Woodland Scenics fine static grass and a Noch Gras-Master applicator. As for autumn crops, with Busch plastic corn rows and some tan paint, you can easily model a cornfield that is waiting to be harvested.

As you put the finishing touches on your fall scenery, consider placing a few figures who are raking leaves. It's a great touch that will immediately make a connection with visitors to your

13-1

Photos by the author

CHAPTER THIRTEEN    by David Popp

# Nature's fireworks

**Trees don't all change color at once, especially in early autumn. I modeled a variety of tree colors found during fall on my N scale Naugatuck Valley layout.**

Next to spring, autumn provides the best opportunity to model some of nature's most dramatic foliage. When I was looking for a season for my N scale layout set in Connecticut's Naugatuck River valley, the tree-covered hillsides of the region just begged to be modeled in the colorful splendor of autumn, **13-1**. Not having built a model railroad with a fall theme before, I decided that it would be a fun challenge.

**13-2**

Plastic tree trunks often have some flashing on them from the molding process. You can clean this off with a sharp hobby knife and remove unwanted armature parts with a sprue nipper.

**13-3**

Shiny, brown plastic tree trunks cry out "fake tree here!" Painting them a flat dark gray is a great quick fix, especially if you want to photograph your layout.

**13-4**

A quick way to vary solid-color, ready-made autumn trees is to stipple the ground-foam foliage with acrylic paint.

**13-5**

This highlighting technique can also be used on green trees as well. Keep in mind that a little paint goes a long way.

**13-6**

After misting the tree with Woodland Scenics Scenic Cement, sprinkle on a lighter shade of ground foam to add color and texture.

**13-7**

This green tree has had foam highlights added, which are more delicate than the paint-stippled highlights.

Regardless of the season you chose, a layout can eat up a lot of trees in a hurry. Even my modest-sized N scale hills were going to require hundreds of trees for a realistic look. While I enjoy the artistry of handcrafted model trees, and indeed that's what I used for many of the foreground trees on my railroad, building a layout full of highly detailed trees isn't practical. So I came up with a few tricks to improve the appearance of inexpensive ready-made trees to quickly cover the background hillsides.

Ready-made trees, in general, tend to be manufactured in one solid color of ground foam. Real trees, however, have a variety of colors. The undersides of leaves tend to be a lighter shade than the surfaces that face the sun, a fact that is recognizable on a windy day. Also, the branch and leaf structures of real trees are open and fluid with motion in the slightest breeze, which allows for many shading variations when viewed in sunlight. These features are noticeably lacking in many modeled trees.

While model trees covered with darker shades of green ground foam

look reasonably well on a model railroad, especially if lighter and darker trees are intermixed when planting a grove of them, the bright colors of autumn trees do not. Because there is little variation in texture, shadow, and color, trees covered in solid yellows, reds, and oranges look cartoonish and unrealistic, which detracts from a scene instead of enhancing it.

If you take a look at most autumn trees, you'll find that they really are not a solid color. Leaves that turn yellow will still have hints of green in them. Those that turn orange will likely have some yellow, and even deep red leaves will have some green, brown, and orange tints. And most leaves in a given tree will not turn color at the same time—many retain patches of green while the rest of the tree has become colorful.

Another point to consider is that unless you're modeling a region of the country that has a predominant type of tree, such as all aspens or birches, the average tree-covered hillside will contain a mixture of species. This means that not all the trees in a wood will be the same color, size, or shape.

Like most other modeling projects, research will help you find the right tree-look for your layout. While first-hand experience is good, photographs are your best source. Since it may be months or years before you get around to adding fall trees to your layout, keeping photos on hand provides a ready reference.

I've included half-a-dozen easy projects for enhancing autumn tree scenes. I've used all of these tips at some point on my own model railroad, but even using just two or three of them will greatly enhance the appearance of your fall scenery. I've also included a short list of sources for ready-made trees in autumn colors.

## Improving trunks and branches

When working with ready-made trees that use plastic armatures, there are two quick fixes that will greatly improve their appearance. First, remove any flashing or unwanted molding nubs from the trunk with a sharp hobby knife, **13-2**. It will probably take you less than 5 seconds to clean up each tree trunk. If there are unwanted

**13-8**

Woodland Scenics Fine Leaf Foliage is a natural, dried product with ground-foam leaves applied to it. Clip several small sprigs from the main stalk to use to build up ready-made trees.

**13-9**

You can attach small branches of the Fine Leaf Foliage to a regular Woodland Scenics ready-made tree using tweezers and white glue.

branches on the tree, you can remove those using a sprue nipper.

The other trunk improvement is to paint it. Shiny, brown plastic has a way of showing up in photographs of your layout when you least expect it, so now's the time to paint the trunk. I use Polly Scale Union Pacific Dark Gray for most tree trunks, **13-3**. If I'm painting birch trees, I use Polly Scale Reefer White and, once the white has dried, I'll add some black marks. Although you can airbrush the trunks, painting them with a brush is just as fast.

## Adding quick color highlights

There are several techniques you can use to break up the solid-color appearance of ready-made trees, as well as give the impression that the trees are in the process of changing color. The easiest one is applying acrylic paint to the ground-foam tree canopy.

I used inexpensive acrylic hobby paints in several autumn colors to augment the color of the foam found on the trees, **13-4**. I poured a small amount of acrylic paint in a plastic container, and then I stippled the tree foliage with the paint, using a 1" disposable foam paintbrush.

I used this technique on an assortment of trees that would be in the scene's background. On some bright yellow trees, I stippled them with an autumn orange color to make it look as though the trees were going to turn a darker shade later. On other yellow trees, I used a lime-green paint to show

that these trees were still in the process of changing to yellow. I also added some lime green to green trees to give the appearance that these trees were beginning to change.

One thing to remember with this technique is that a little paint goes a long way, **13-5**. You're trying to create a suggestion of color variation, not repaint the entire tree, so don't get too heavy handed when stippling the ground foam.

## Highlighting with ground foam

Another technique you can use on solid-color trees is highlighting the canopy with fine ground foam. After misting the tree with diluted matte medium or Woodland Scenics Scenic Cement, sprinkle on fine ground foam in a shade that is lighter than the tree's original color, **13-6**. This technique also adds texture to the tree.

While this technique takes more time, the end result is a more delicate appearance than the paint-stippled highlights, **13-7**, and it works best on green trees. As with the painted trees, however, go sparingly on the highlights. Too much highlighted color will make the tree look two-tone, which is not the desired effect.

## Detailing branches

So far, I've covered projects that show how to enhance background trees. However, here's an easy tip you can use to make good-looking foreground trees with minimal effort.

Woodland Scenics makes a product called Fine Leaf Foliage, **13-8**. This is a natural material that has been dried and had ground foam leaves added to it. You can use the foliage as brush or glue it to traditional plastic or wire trunk armatures to make larger, delicate-looking trees. You can also use it to enhance ready-made trees.

Start by selecting a color of the foliage material that is close to the color of the tree you wish to augment. Next, clip several small sprigs of the foliage. Grab one of the sprigs with a tweezers and dip the end of the branch in white glue. Then select a spot on the ready-made tree where a branch might grow and insert the end of the sprig into the foam tree canopy, **13-9**. Since you are building more canopy on top of the existing tree, it will take you a bit of practice to get the proper tree shape.

Once the white glue has dried, you can trim the foliage sprigs to improve the shape of the tree. The end result is a tree that has already lost some of its leaves and reveals some internal branch structure. You can further reinforce this effect by placing some ground-foam leaves of a similar color on the ground under the tree after you plant it on the layout, **13-10**.

## Grouping trees by color

Planting your autumn trees in a realistic fashion takes as much thought as creating the trees themselves. Again, unless you're modeling a region of the country that is predominated by one or two spe-

**13-10**

The finished result is a tree that has already lost some of its leaves, which you can reinforce by sprinkling a few foam leaves of the same color on the ground under the tree.

**13-11**

A forest is often made up of mini-groves of similar trees, so try planting three or four trees of the same color near each other, such as these yellow and orange trees are.

**13-12**

You can enhance the appearance of your autumn forest by using clumps of ground foam as brush around the perimeter of a wood. Here, I've used various colors of Woodland Scenics Foliage Clusters to make the wood seem bigger.

**13-13**

Once the basic forest is in place, you can add a few finely detailed "hero" trees to the mix. Like branch-detailed trees, hero trees break up the impression of trees made from solid foam.

cies of trees, such as a mountain valley grove of aspens, you'll want to provide a mix of tree colors in your scene.

Trees tend to grow in clusters or mini-groves within a forest, **13-11**. While there may still be an intermingling of trees in a particular stand, you can achieve realistic results by planting three to five trees of the same color near each other and then surround them with several groups of different trees. Tree seeds often grow near where they came from, so tree groups will have one or two large parent trees and several smaller offspring around them. However, animals and birds can help spread tree seeds, so one or more interloper trees will commonly be present in a stand as well. The important thing is not to work in a predictable pattern of colors and sizes.

Adding shrubs and scrub growth around your trees magnifies the trees' impact, **13-12**. This growth represents the young trees and various bushes along the edges of a wood. By using materials of similar color and texture as those you've used for your trees, you can give the impression that the forest is really much larger than it is. At the edge of a tree line, I added Woodland Scenics Foliage Clusters, and these clusters make it seem like there are more trees on the hill than there really are.

## Planting hero trees

After you've planted the bulk of the forest, add a few super-detailed trees called "hero trees" to give the scene extra interest, **13-13**. Hero trees are those that have very fine detail, making

them visually much more interesting than trees used in background areas.

Trees lose their leaves at different times, and in any autumn forest, you can have trees that are full color, bare, still green, and partially leafed all at the same time. Most of the trees we've worked on up to this point are either fully or partially leafed, so let's look at a few ways to add sparse and bare trees to the scene. Since these trees are the most delicate that we'll add to the finished scene, they are our hero trees.

For sparse trees, I like to use Scenic Express SuperTrees kits. These trees use a natural material for armatures, **13-14**. After soaking the armatures in diluted matte medium and letting them dry, you can airbrush them with a dark-gray acrylic paint. Once the paint is dry, you can cover the armatures with your choice

13-14

Scenic Express SuperTrees use a natural material armature. After soaking the armature in diluted matte medium and then painting it with acrylic paint, you can cover the armature with as much or as little ground foam as you wish.

13-15

It's best to place hero trees last in the process. This will not only protect these more delicate trees, but it will allow you to position them so they can be used to the best advantage in a scene.

13-16

All woods have trees that have either lost their leaves early or are simply dead. Planting a few finely detailed bare trees, such as these wire armatures by the N Scale Architect, will add to the realism of your forest.

## Autumn tree suppliers

### Grand Central Gems
Ready-made aspen, oak, and sage oak offered in fall colors

### Scenic Express
SuperTrees kits include assorted fall foliage colors in several scales
Ready-made trees with plastic armatures offered in two autumn colors

### Timberline Scenery Co.
Ready-made late autumn trees having wood trunks with wire armatures in assorted colors

### Woodland Scenics
Ready-made bulk Trees Value Packs of fall trees with plastic armatures in three different sizes and four colors
Premium Trees include maple and beech trees with wire armatures in fall colors

of ground foam. Since these trees have a delicate texture, I use very little ground foam, simulating trees that are almost finished with their autumn change.

In building the forest scene, I add the SuperTrees last because they are delicate and shouldn't be handled or bumped much. I place the SuperTrees randomly around the tree canopy, usually slightly above the tree line, **13-15**.

Bare trees are another detail to consider for a forest scene. These trees are either dead, or in the case of an autumn scene, may have already finished the leaf cycle, **13-16**. You can use a natural material like SuperTrees for bare trees, or you can use fine wire or brass tree armatures. My bare trees are made from brass armatures by the N Scale Architect. Bare trees are also considered to be hero trees, and I've placed them slightly above the rest of the tree canopy so they draw attention.

You don't need a lot of hero trees in a given scene, but a few make great accents. And these better-detailed trees leave viewers believing that your forest has more depth and texture than it really does.

Photos by the author

CHAPTER FOURTEEN    by Horst Meier

# Easy autumn trees

Autumn is my favorite time of year as well as the setting of my HO scale model railroad. Assembled tree models and scenery material are available in several autumn colors, but I've found that using these products straight out of the package doesn't look very realistic. The colors look too uniform, without the variations found in nature.

I use Heki tree models (301-305) covered with Noch mini-leaves, **14-1**. Both Heki and Noch are well-known European model scenery manufacturers. I place Heki Super Artline trees in the foreground of my layout and less-detailed trees in the background, where they are less visible.

Using Noch mini-leaves colored with acrylic paint washes, I modeled this realistic autumn setting on my HO scale Union Pacific layout.

14-2

Autumn foliage is found in a wide range of subtle shades, from green to red and orange.

14-3

Add a package of your preferred foliage and the paint wash to a plastic container.

14-4

Spread the colored foliage in a box and stir the leaves with a spatula so they dry.

14-5

Spray each tree with clear matte finish so the foliage sticks to the tree.

14-6

To obtain subtler shades, roll the trees in light green foliage and then in an autumn mix.

14-7

For just a light showing of fall color, sprinkle foliage onto a tree using a shaker jar.

Using acrylic paint washes, I can color the foliage of my trees in a seemingly endless variety of browns, greens, oranges, yellows, and reds. Follow along as I show you how to quickly and easily give the foliage on your layout a full palette of realistic autumn colors, **14-2**.

## Coloring the foliage

I use six colors of Noch mini-leaves for my trees, including olive green (7140), light green (7142), medium green (7144), dark green (7146), yellow (7148), and red (7149). You can use all of one color, or you can mix the colors together to create more varied tones. The final foliage color depends on the acrylic paint wash. You can layer as many different colors of foliage as you like. I've found it most effective to mix contrasting shades, such as pale green and orange. Photos of real trees, especially those located along your favorite prototype railroad, are useful color guides.

For fall foliage, I use brown, orange, red, and yellow acrylic paints. I also use green paint to tone down the red and yellow foliage. I mix a wash of each color, using a ratio of two parts paint to

one part water. I also add two or three drops of dishwashing liquid to each wash, which helps the color better penetrate the foliage material.

You can apply the wash to the foliage using a plastic container having a lid. Covered paint or coffee cans also work well. First, put a package of foliage into the empty container and then pour in about one ounce of the wash color, **14-3**. After making sure that the lid is tightly sealed, vigorously shake the container. Next, remove the lid and stir the foliage with a plastic spatula, making sure to scrape the foliage from the bottom of the container. Then replace the lid and shake the container again.

Washes of different thicknesses produce different effects. For some of my red and yellow leaves, I only want to slightly dull the color, so I'll use a thinner brown wash (three parts water to one part paint).

## Applying the foliage

After applying the wash, dump the foliage into a small cardboard box to dry, **14-4**. Then stir the foliage with a plastic spatula, wait 10 minutes, and

then stir it again. Put the dry foliage into another clean plastic covered container. I combine various colors to make an autumn foliage mix.

At my workbench, I pour a small amount of my autumn mix foliage onto a sheet of white paper. Then, on another sheet of paper, I'll pour some light green foliage. Next, I spray trees, one at a time, with clear matte finish (Testor's Dullcote also works), so the foliage will adhere to them, **14-5**. Then I roll each tree in the foliage. For the background trees, I only use the autumn mix. To color the foreground trees, I first roll them in light green foliage, spray them lightly again with clear matte finish, and then roll them in the autumn mix, **14-6**. Rolling them in the light green foliage first results in a more subtle final shade.

To add a bit of early autumn color to a green tree, you can add small patches of color, **14-7**. Put your foliage mix in a container having a shaker lid and simply sprinkle on the appropriately colored foliage.

*(First appeared in* Model Railroader *November 2009)*

CHAPTER FIFTEEN    by Paul J. Dolkos

# The leafless season

Model railroad scenery can be a vast sea of green. Often in summer settings, dry patches of grass or even dead trees are seldom seen. It's a horticulturist's dream. But in some regions, it may be six months between the time leaves fall and green ones reappear. Late fall, winter, and early spring landscape is seldom the basis for model railroad scenery, but their leafless look can be very dramatic, **15-1**.

A Barre & Chelsea mixed train crosses the Boston & Maine at Wells on my layout. A mix of conifers and deciduous trees is used in front of the plain blue backdrop. Woodland Scenics foliage netting represents vegetation on the hillside on the right.

15-2

A bramble-filled and weed-grown slope with a fall look is created by using layers of various types of vegetation. Keep adding bits and pieces until it has the look of the unkept real estate that it is. Depending on the region being depicted, some green might added, representing low-growing evergreen vines or shrubs.

15-3

Leafless trees let viewer look through and into a scene, such as this one, where you can see a driveway to a passenger station.

15-4

This hillside shows how it takes more than just some leafless trees to create a late fall or winter scene. During this time, it is much easier to see under and through the trees, so make sure to cover the ground with ground-up leaves and fallen branches.

Many years ago, when I began to scenic my Boston & Maine-themed model railroad, I thought materials like lichen and balls of poly fiber commonly used for replicating foliage left something to be desired. So I reasoned why not try to model a season that features trees without leaves. Also in the back of my mind was the idea that this would give the layout a distinctive look. Although today, there is a wider and improved choice of model foliage materials available, modeling the leafless season remains an interesting scenery alternative.

Modeling this time of year requires more than just creating some trees without leaves. The ground cover includes dormant bushes, grasses, and fallen leaves. 15-2. It has a brown hue, perhaps with a dash of red, and some green vines here and there. Most deciduous trees lose their leaves, but a few varieties, such as oaks, retain some leaves although they have turned brown. Conifers, or pines remain green throughout the year. So there is a range of vegetation shapes and colors, some peculiar to specific regions, which can be incorporated into a leafless fall or winter scene.

I decided to set my New England railroad scene in November. This, I reasoned, justified the leafless trees but without having to model snow. (November snows are not uncommon in New England, but a snowpack usually does not accumulate.) While snow would have added another nice scenic touch, I simply decided that it was an element I didn't want to include.

Being able to see through the leafless trees has disadvantages as well as advantages when modeling a layout. With leafless trees, it's harder to create an effective view block if you want to hide a track running off scene, but the strategic placement of evergreens will solve that problem. On the other hand, being able to watch trains run through a grove of bare trees adds interest for viewers, 15-3.

## Starting with a scenery base

Regardless of the season modeled, you need to start with a scenery base. There are many ways to create a layout's terrain base, including a plaster shell. However, I prefer extruded polystyrene insulation sheet material, often referred to as the pink (Owens Corning) or blue (Dow) stuff. You can easily cut or sculpt the polystyrene insulation to a desired form, although you should keep a shop vacuum on hand if you don't want to cover your railroad with shavings. Still, it's easier to clean up than messy plaster.

With an insulation base, an advantage in making fall and winter scenery is that you can easily poke a pilot hole into the insulation and insert a tree or even a delicate bush. The material's thickness supports the vegetation firmly without glue. If you want to remove and reposition a tree, simply pull it out, poke another hole, and reinsert the tree. To plant trees and bushes in plaster, you'd have to drill a hole, which creates white dust. And since the plaster is usually just a thin shell, which provides little or no support for the trunk, a tree would probably have to be glued in place.

Once the insulation is shaped and smoothed, I usually paint it an earth color and scatter some foam, fine dirt granules, or other scenic texturing material on the paint while it is still wet. Then you're ready to begin detailing.

## Detailing the ground

Especially for the leafless season, because you can see into the forest, it's best to first apply the desired ground cover before planting model trees, **15-4**. Once the trees are installed, it is more difficult to access the area under them. The amount of vegetation underneath a tree canopy varies and may be limited because the light is blocked. But often you will find brambles and vines that can be replicated using foliage netting. Fallen branches are also common. For these, scatter pieces of weed stems and twigs. Finally, sprinkle a layer of ground-up leaves to represent the accumulation of leaves under the trees over the years. Of course, these leaves are present no matter what season you are depicting. Generally being a light brown, fallen leaves add a bit of brightness to the scene.

On the left are ground up or pulverized leaves that make an ideal forest ground cover. Pulverize them in a kitchen blender as you would vegetables or crush them in your hand and then sift them though a screen to remove stems and oversized pieces.

The reddish bushes are Woodland Scenics fall foliage toned down with a light spray of brown.

A mixture of pines and deciduous trees provides an effective scenery transition between the track and backdrop. Behind this narrow strip, a mountain outline painted on the backdrop, although somewhat obscured by the trees, suggests that the scene extends onward.

**15-8**

To create a leafless tree, a web of fine branches should be added to the basic frame. Here, baby's breath stems have already been glued on. Scenic Express SuperTrees pieces, such as the one held by the tweezers, are ideal branch materials.

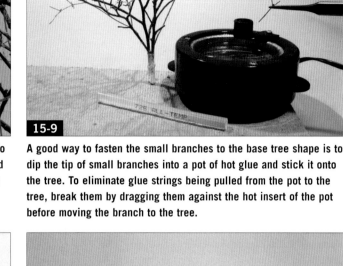

**15-9**

A good way to fasten the small branches to the base tree shape is to dip the tip of small branches into a pot of hot glue and stick it onto the tree. To eliminate glue strings being pulled from the pot to the tree, break them by dragging them against the hot insert of the pot before moving the branch to the tree.

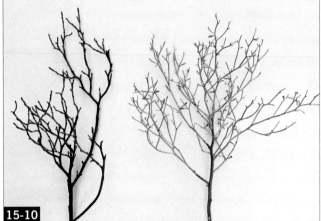

**15-10**

These 6-8" twigs are an ideal configuration for model leafless trees. The branch pattern is fairly tight as compared to much natural growth where branch junctions are further apart.

**15-11**

On the left is a tree armature where two twigs have been glued together at the base to form a multi-trunk tree. In the middle, plaster has been applied to the trunks to make a single-trunk tree and give the base some bulk. On the right is a completed tree with fine branches added. It has been sprayed to blend everything together.

To create fallen leaves, grind up dry tree leaves in a blender or just crumble them up in your hand, which is a more time-consuming technique, **15-5**. Whenever I mention using a blender to pulverize leaves, people question the advisability of this, but it is no different than using it with any other type of vegetable matter. Just wash out the blender as you would after any other use. If you used any water during the pulverizing process, let the leaves dry out. Then sift the leaves through window-sized or similar screening to remove stems and veins. Scatter and affix the leaves with white glue as you would with ballast.

With commercial ground cover material, you'll find that there is a limited range of appropriate colors for the fall. Often the colors, such as red or yellow, are too bright or of a shade unknown in nature. So to tone things down, I lightly spray the material with brown paint, **15-6**. If you don't try to change the color of some scenery materials, you really limit yourself on what you can do with fall and winter scenery.

Some model railroaders may shy away from fall and winter scenery because it seems so gray and bleak. And, indeed, I have noted that in some regions there is little color other than brown and gray. So when modeling

these scenes, if it's appropriate, you can introduce evergreen bushes and trees for a little variation, **15-7**. Also, bright tungsten lighting, as opposed to fluorescents, creates interesting shadows and adds sparkle.

## Creating leafless deciduous trees

My first woodland leafless scenery efforts began by simply inserting tree-like twigs into a Styrofoam scenery form that I had covered with winter-hued ground cover. I used twigs and weeds that had as many branches as possible to create a thicket. When you look at a grove of trees, you'll notice that the spacing is quite close; in fact,

**15-12**

As an alternative to store-bought plants, you can harvest the flowers and seed pods from the tops of weeds during fall. These items are a good source of upright ground cover detail. Often, they can be trimmed to any desired size and used without any further painting or preservation treatment.

**15-13**

To create a pine from an armature made from an artificial Christmas tree (left to right): trim to the shape and size desired, spray with adhesive and sprinkle on fine foam, apply another light coat of adhesive and sprinkle on flocking, and spray it dark green.

much closer than you can normally plant individual model trees. In a forest, as trees grow, their branches intertwine with neighboring trees, which we don't or can't model. So to create this look, I inserted straight twigs without any branches through the canopy. The fact that these tree trunks had no upper branches was disguised by the twigs with branches. While, in general, I thought this modeling was satisfactory, I didn't think the overall look of the branch structure was good. On the other hand, I never replaced the trees in this scene, and this approach could be used to create a grove behind more detailed model trees.

The next step for me was to develop a way to efficiently create individual tree models. The first consideration is the basic tree armature. For an earlier layout, I had built some from twisted picture-hanging wire painted with latex rubber to give the trunk and branches some bulk. Using twisted wire for armatures allows you to create the shape of a specific species, perhaps where you want to have a stand-alone specimen on a lawn or along a road. Originally, my wire armatures had been used with lichen for summer trees and had no fine branches.

To create the small branches of a bare canopy, I first used baby's breath, also called gypsophila, after removing the blossoms, **15-8**. Today, most of the baby's breath sold commercially has

been treated with a preservative, making the blossoms difficult to remove. So using untreated material is recommended. An alternative material I now use is SuperTrees natural growth, which is imported and sold by Scenic Express. Both large and small pieces can be used to build the fine upper tree limbs.

To fasten the fine branches to the base armature, I first used white glue but later discovered hot glue was faster and easier, **15-9**. I dip the branch stem into a warming pot (sold by craft stores) of melted hot glue and place it where desired. Admittedly, this approach is a bit tedious, so you want to build these in small groups of six or so. Once the top of the trees are filled out to your satisfaction with enough fine branches, spray the tree a dark gray or brownish gray. A spray can of primer works well.

I was looking for a more efficient way to produce armatures than by twisting them out of wire, so I started examining natural growth. The problem with a lot of natural growth is that the individual branches are too far apart. You want to find a branch pattern that is very compact, **15-10**. Generally, low-growing plants have more potential to yield this type of material.

I can't recommend any specific variety because I've been unable to identify any of the wild plants I use. Also, vegetation is so diverse from region to region and species so varied that naming

something won't really help. So if you're looking for armature material, whenever you're outside, examine the local vegetation, particularly its stem structure.

Ultimately, I did find some plant stems that were satisfactory for armatures. Note that I didn't say perfect, but they do provide a good representation of generic trees. I sometimes hot-glue additional heavier branches to the armature or break a branch to reset it at a more pleasing angle. Often the trunk is too thin. This can be ignored, but you can also bundle one or two additional twigs together to increase the girth, **15-11**. You can leave the bundled twigs as is to represent a multi-trunk tree or apply plaster or another filler material to make it into a single large trunk. Another issue with natural material is that by trimming the armatures, you can create unattractive, blunt limb ends, which sometimes you can hide with fine branch material.

To flesh out a scene with hand-built trees, check out the dried flower selection at craft or florist supply stores. They offer heather, sugar bush, gypsy blooms, and many other items that are useful either as background trees or small bushes, **15-12**. For fall and winter scenes you'll want to remove the blossoms from some of these plants and probably paint them.

A word about model tree sizes: generally, we make our trees are too small. It is not uncommon for mature trees to grow 100 feet or taller. Most model trees are scaled less than half that. While a model tree scaled to 100 feet or more would be a foot tall, and since our eyes are accustomed to shorter trees, it would look out of place on most layouts. But, nevertheless, we should think about prototype tree heights, and as we scenic our railroads, remember to include taller specimens.

## Making pine trees

Like a deciduous tree, creating a conifer requires finding a satisfactory armature. Very usable are the bottlebrush variety, which can purchased in many sizes. For larger trees or spots where I want to fill out a background I've used pieces of an artificial Christmas tree as armatures, **15-13**. But these artificial armatures usually need additional work to get rid of their dime-store look.

I found an excellent way to have an endless supply of pine tree armatures. One day in a nursery shop, I spotted a houseplant called a foxtail fern, **15-14**. It features upright branches that look to me like miniature conifers, **15-15**. During warm months, I keep the plant outside and during the winter sheltered inside. In subtropical climates, it can be grown outside year-round. So any time I need some pine trees, I just clip a few branches. To preserve them and dress up the fronds requires a little work.

With either the fern or bottlebrush armatures, I trim them to the desired size and apply a light coating of spray adhesive, which is best done outside. You don't want sticky overspray covering your workspace. Sprinkle on some fine foam ground cover such as Woodland Scenics fine turf. This adds bulk and texture to the branches, and the adhesive keeps the fern's leaves from falling off as it dries out.

Next, spray a second light coat of adhesive on the armature and sprinkle on some flocking (short strands of fiber, not ground rubber foam which is sometimes also called flocking) using a shaker container. The flocking gives the trees a fuzzy look, which you would expect when looking at a needle-filled pine tree. The color of the foam and flocking does not matter because the

15-14

**You can grow your own model conifers. The fronds of the foxtail fern provide an endless supply of pine tree armatures.**

15-15

**Pines made using foxtail fern branches have a nice open look compared to those made from bottlebrush armatures.**

15-16

**At left is a pine with foam and flocking before being painted and, at right, is another after painting and final trimming.**

last step is to spray the tree a dark pine green, **15-16**.

One caution is to not apply too much adhesive, foam, or flocking. Overdoing it can cause the materials to clump up on the armature. Hair spray could be substituted as a less aggressive adhesive. The process goes very quickly, and you can produce a number of pines in a short period.

## Producing chills

I am very happy with the decision to model the late fall-winter season with its leafless trees. It indeed gave my layout a distinctive look, although one friend always says when he visits, "I hate when the leaves fall, and I know the cold weather is coming soon. Your railroad makes me shiver." I guess I got it right!

16-1

CHAPTER SIXTEEN    by Lance Mindheim

# Harvested crop fields

The roots of our country's economy literally sprang from an agricultural base, and the presence of the agricultural scene throughout America continues to this day. For many model railroad themes, what could look more fitting than a train slicing across vast vistas of crop fields? Whether your layout is set in Maryland, California, or Illinois, adding some expansive agriculture fields to your scenery will go a long way toward setting the scene, **16-1**.

A Monon southbound local crosses barren winter crop fields just south of Bloomington, Ind., on my N scale layout.

16-2

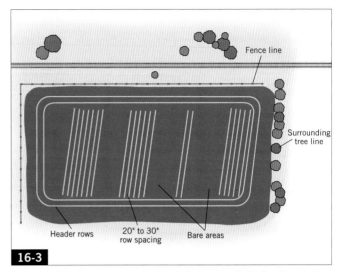

16-3

On October 28, 1977, Amtrak's southbound *Floridian* crosses a harvested corn field filled with partial stalks. Note the amber color of the stalks, bare patches in the field, and the tree lines in the distance.

This drawing shows a common layout for a corn field. Angling the rows in relation to the tracks gives the field a more interesting look. Note the bare areas, fence lines, and tree line.

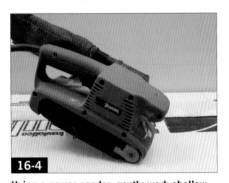

16-4

Using a power sander, gently work shallow undulations into the foam scenery base.

16-5

After forming the ground contours, paint the foam an earth tone with diluted acrylic paint.

16-6

Prior to sprinkling on your earth scenery material, paint on a thin coat of white glue.

As the seasons roll by, these fields transition from bare earth to sprouting crops, full grown plants, and finally harvested crops. We've all seen the results at the end of the cycle represented by acres of dark earth stripped of their cash crop. However, not all crops are harvested, and even if they are, vestiges remain throughout late fall and winter. During these months, you will notice many amber fields with full or partial crop stalks still standing, **16-2**. Modeling a barren-earth crop field would be simple enough. However, including an occasional harvested field containing some standing plants is certainly prototypical and adds an element of interest.

Regardless of the season being modeled, representing fields of crops in model form does require some thought. Do you model individual plants or go for a general representation? The answer usually lies in how large the field is that is being modeled. Modeling individual plants makes sense if you're representing a small garden or just a small portion of a larger field. There are some excellent products on the market to model individual crop plants, some even found in etched brass. While these individual plant products are well suited to a small foreground scene, planting them in vast numbers in an expansive field becomes too time-intensive and costly to be practical.

For larger fields, another method needs to be employed that will create a plausible representation without taking an overwhelming number of hours to build. The human eye is very sensitive to color, texture, and shapes. If we can model these elements correctly and add a few detailed crops here and there, the brain is fooled into thinking it is looking at a fully detailed field. Let's take a look at how we can create a plausible repre-

sentation of a relatively large field with late fall or winter crops.

Before you get started, take a quick look at an actual field during the season, **16-3**. Take note of the vegetation that springs up at the fence lines, the occasional bare spots, and the header rows bordering the field (used to enable farmers to turn their tractors when they get to the end of the row). Don't spend a lot of time focusing on the actual crop-row spacing but rather set a spacing that looks reasonable to the eye such as ¼" to ⅜". In the real world, there is no firm distance for corn-row spacing, although the historical trend has been toward narrower and narrower rows. At the turn of the 20th century, 36" to 40" spacing was the norm, but in more recent times, you may find spacing as narrow as 24".

In the model world, creating row distances tighter than ¼" becomes somewhat difficult and impractical.

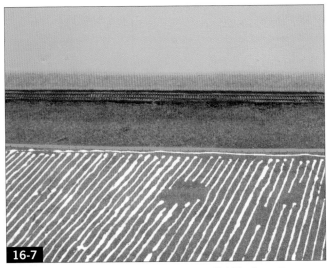

16-7

Lay beads of full-strength white glue on your field in the pattern you chose for your particular crop. A steel rule helps keep the rows straight. Be sure to allow breaks in the glue lines to represent bare areas in the field. In this photo, the beads are about ¼" apart.

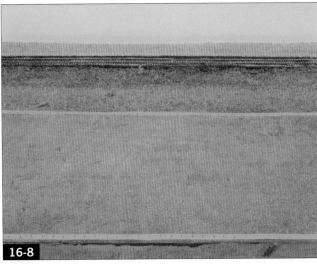

16-8

Laying masking tape with hash marks along the edge of your field can help keep your crop rows evenly spaced.

16-9

After you've sprinkled the static grass over your glue lines, use a steel rule to gently force some of the grass into the glue. Doing so will give your rows a thicker, fuller look.

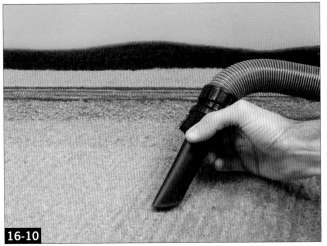

16-10

Once the glue beads have completely dried, vacuum up the excess static grass.

## Making a soil base

Even a field that appears to be billiard-table smooth, upon further examination, will have some undulations. As with most of my scenery, I use extruded foam as the base. To create the effect of slight undulations in the ground, take a power sander and, using a light touch, gently work some very shallow dips into the foam base, **16-4**. Shoot for a depth of no more than ⅟₁₆" to ⅛". Be sure to wear a respirator while sanding the foam. After you've worked some shallow undulations into the foam, paint it a neutral shade of a brown earth color with diluted acrylic craft paint, **16-5**. Next comes the earth base for the field.

Smear a very thin layer of white glue over the field area, **16-6**. Using brown soil material, such as Arizona Rock and Mineral Company Earth, sprinkle on your dirt, being careful that there are no blobs or thin spots. Gently wet the soil with a fine mist of water and a splash of alcohol. Finally, gently drip on a mix of 25 percent white glue (or matte medium), 75 percent water, and a touch of alcohol. Let your wet soil dry.

## Adding dead crops

After your soil base has dried, you can start adding the dead crops. As mentioned, the exact spacing is not critical as long as you keep the rows parallel and roughly ¼" to ⅜" apart. The overall look of dead crops will be represented by sprinkling beige static grass onto beads of white glue. Begin with the header rows and lay several lines of glue around the borders of the field, **16-7**. Next, lay the glue beads down for the parallel crop rows. Angling the rows in relation to the fascia or the tracks adds an element of interest. Be sure to leave gaps in your glue lines to represent bare soil patches. Using a steel rule as a guide is helpful in keeping the rows of glue beads straight. Another useful guide is laying a strip of thin masking tape at the end of the rows and marking the row spacing on the tape with a marker, **16-8**.

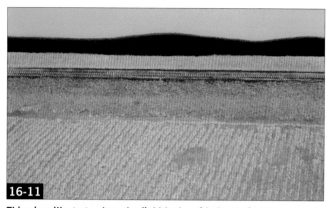

**16-11**

This view illustrates how the field looks with the static grass embedded in the glue lines.

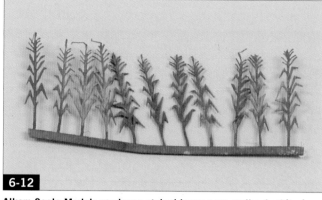

**6-12**

Alkem Scale Models produces etched brass corn stalks. In this view, the stalks have been painted a neutral beige, and the strips cut into strips 1-2" long.

**16-13**

To insert the etched stalks in the furrow, cut a small slot with a hobby knife and insert the brass strip into the slot with tweezers.

**16-14**

A touch of color is provided by some evergreens and green weeds.

After you've laid down all of your glue lines, take Heki 2mm Static Prairie Grass (no. 3363) to represent the dried crops. Using a shaker bottle or static grass applicator, liberally cover all of your glue lines. To make sure that you have firmly seated the grass into the glue line, gently push some of the grass into the glue with the edge of a steel rule or knife, **16-9**. Do not spray the sprinkled-on static grass with a wetting agent as that will dilute your glue lines and cause them to run. After you've covered the entire field with static grass, let the white glue fully dry. When you are satisfied that the glue has dried, vacuum up the excess static grass, which leaves your exposed crop lines, **16-10**. Now, apply a fixative to the crop rows to ensure they stay in place. Extra-hold hair spray or a 1:4 matte medium and water mix works well. If some of the rows are not as full as you would like, you can patch them by laying another glue line in the bare area and using a pair of tweezers to plant additional clumps of static grass.

## Detailing the crops

At this point, the field itself would be fine as is, **16-11**. If you desire a slightly more detailed look, additional texture can be added by inserting some more detailed crops here and there. Alkem Scale Models makes some beautiful etched brass cornstalks, **16-12**. The Alkem stalks come in long strips on an etched fret. Spray the brass Alkem stalks a neutral beige color. I generally purchase inexpensive spray paints in suitable earth colors. Highlight the ends of the stalks by dry-brushing on browns or grays. When using the Alkem stalks, I generally snip the strips into shorter sections of five or six stalks. To plant the brass stalks into the field, run an hobby knife into your crop furrow to make a small cut and then insert your corn strip into the slot, **16-13**. Afterward, bend a few stalks over, and twisting the stalks gives you more of a 3-D look.

## Finalizing the borders

Once the field has been completed, the last area to detail is the area bordering the field. While the field itself may be relatively well groomed, the vegetation leading up to the field often is not. Start by bordering your field with a fence line. Use N or HO scale lumber to represent typical 4 x 4 posts (see Chapter Six). Next work in some taller grass, scrub, and short trees (10 to 15 scale feet tall) parallel to the fence line. Finally, scatter some fully mature hardwood trees along the fence line. Even in winter, not everything is totally brown, so add some evergreens and patches of green weeds here and there, **16-14**.

This relatively simple method of creating harvested crop fields goes quickly enough so that creating larger expanses of open fields becomes more practical. The end result has enough texture to create a plausible representation of one of the more common elements found beside a railroad right-of-way during late fall and winter.

17-1

CHAPTER SEVENTEEN    by Mike Danneman

# Fall backdrop tips

The best advice I can give you about painting an autumn backdrop is to keep the colors subtle. Although autumn trees are noted for flaming red, yellow, and orange colors, **17-1**, many times these colors are not as intense as you may think. Not all varieties of trees sport brilliant colors as red and sugar maples do. Elms and some oaks just turn brown, while others, such as black walnut trees, remain green. Also, not all trees turn color at the same time. Many factors such as rainfall, temperature, and soil affect the tall colors of trees, and colors can vary in shades and intensity from year to year, **17-2**.

A Conrail freight works its way west through famous Horseshoe Curve in Pennsylvania on October 21, 1988. Note the kaleidoscope of colors in the background hills. Even on the most spectacular autumn days, don't forget that not all the trees change colors at the same time, and you should include green foliage too.

17-2

Many time the colors of autumn are just not that intense. A Chicago and North Western freight heads west through North Lake, Wis., on October 18, 1992, through the soft fall colors of a Midwestern autumn.

17-3

In this view of a CSX train at Mance, Penn., on October 22, 1988, note how the bright autumn colors in the trees become more muted in the background. The autumn colors you paint on your backdrop should be more subtle than your foreground trees.

17-4

A Norfolk Southern coal train is westbound at Montgomery, Va., on October 24, 1990. The fall colors are subtle, and even though the background mountains are covered with autumn foliage, they appear bluish. This blue tone pushes the distant mountains back, making them look even more distant.

17-5

Union Pacific No. 6858 pilots a coal train exiting the Moffat Tunnel. Sparkling yellow aspens rim the mountain side. Due to the joint structure of their root systems, aspen trees are always grouped in clumps, which is how they should seen on a backdrop.

Those brilliant reds, oranges, and yellows that usually grace many of our deciduous trees each autumn will have their colors muted by distance, 17-3. Humidity, smoke, and particulates in the air give everything in the distance a much more subtle color, 17-4. This factor should be even truer when it comes to painting a backdrop. It is always a great idea to view some photographs of the area you are modeling to observe the colors.

If you are modeling the Midwest, autumn is also harvest time, so most fields will have a gold or yellow color. Trees lining the bountiful farm fields will still be green or slowly changing into autumn colors, belying the end of another growing season.

In some of the mountainous Western states, brilliant, golden aspens light up the hillsides, 17-5. On your backdrop, these bright yellow colors should also be toned down to suggest the appearance of distance.

Remember, if the colors are too hard to believe, then they probably are and should be muted to better represent the real thing.

# Winter, crisp and clear

by David Popp

It was a snowy January morning in Genoa, Ill., in the early 1990s. There'd been a major snowstorm the day before, and then the temperature had plummeted to well below zero. The next morning, nasty winds and drifting snow made driving dangerous.

During that period of my life, I was a commuter student, attending Northern Illinois University in DeKalb, and part of my daily driving route took me through the small town of Genoa. The best part of my hour-long drive was that from Genoa through Kingston, where I paralleled the Soo Line's (former Milwaukee Road's) Chicago to Kansas City right-of-way for about 10 miles. That morning, as I approached the railroad tracks at the center of Genoa, I caught the tail end of a Soo Line train heading east toward Chicago, complete with a caboose! I could just make out the guy in the cupola as the car went past in a swirl of snow, and I couldn't help think how lucky I was to have witnessed this classic piece of railroading. (As it turned out, I wasn't entirely lucky that day since NIU had decided to close the school on account of the weather, so I had driven all that way just to turn around and head back home!)

Though winter is my least favorite season, it does offer some dramatic imagery for modeling and photography. The scene shown in the photo is a diorama I'd built several years ago. I used the image of that day in Genoa as the inspiration for the scene.

While building my Genoa diorama, I discovered that modeling a winter scene is actually quite fun and has its own set of scenic challenges. What do you use for snow? Being that snow is white, how do you keep it clean after you've built it? How do you model convincing winter trees and bushes? What do vehicles and structures look like in winter? How do you model snow pushed back by a plow? These were just a few of the things I had to answer when building my 3 x 4-foot diorama, and a lot of its construction was simply done by trial and error. Fortunately, if you decide to add a winter scene to your railroad, there are now a wide variety of products available for modeling convincing winter scenery.

While winter is one of the lesser-modeled seasons, it is still popular because it has great wow factor with visitors. Your entire model railroad does not have to be set in winter either. I've seen a number of layouts that have just one section or one scene placed in a winter setting. Usually it is a mountain section of the layout or an area that is separated from the other parts of the railroad by walls or dividers. The important thing is that there is some way to eliminate awkward transitions between seasons.

So, if you're looking to do something radically different, I encourage you to try winter scenery. Even if you just build a simple diorama for photographs like I did, I think you'll enjoy the challenge.

I modeled this winter scene as a photo diorama. Making winter scenery requires many different skills and materials, and it can be a fun modeling challenge. *Photo by David Popp*

18-1

Photos by the author

CHAPTER EIGHTEEN    by Lance Mindheim

# Shallow rock cuts

**In this winter scene on my N scale layout, the Monon's northbound *Thoroughbred* passes through a narrow rock cut as it approaches the outskirts of Bloomington, Ind.**

As railroads cross the landscape, rarely, if ever, do they have the luxury of traversing perfectly flat terrain. Even when the right-of-way is designed to take the path of least resistance, there will inevitably be dips that must be filled, and shallow rises that must be excavated out of the way. Cuts make for appealing modeling subjects because, as the excavator does his task, whatever geology lies beneath the surface is exposed for viewing. Since shallow rock cuts are such a common element of the railroad landscape adding a few here and there to your model railroad creates an added sense of realism, **18-1**. They add a dramatic touch to any season but especially when combined with stark winter vegetation. Let's take a look at how we can create a common, shallow rock cut.

A good way to begin is by taking a look at some actual rock cuts in the field, **18-2**. When you look at a cut, see if the rock is entirely or partially exposed. Examine how the rock broke away when it was excavated. Is the exposed excavated face comprised of large, blocky angular chunks common with granite, or is it highly stratified with many parallel layers as you would find with limestone or sandstone? Is the face primarily soil with a few outcrops here and there, or is it primarily just rock? Did the rock break away cleanly in large chunks or did it shatter and spall, leaving small rock debris strewn down the face? The geology of the region you are modeling will serve as the best guide in providing this information.

## Forming the cut

When forming the cut, it is often easier to cut the associated landforms from extruded foam on your workbench and then glue them in place on the layout. When shaping the rock faces, try to envision how the soil profile and hill slope would have been shaped prior to being excavated for the railroad right-of-way, **18-3**.

The slope of the rock face and soil bank will vary with geology, but a 30-degree slope on the rock face is a good overall average, **18-4**. Take blocks of foam, cut a rough 30-degree face on them and then contour the remainder of the block into a gently rolling hill. Using a hot wire foam cutter is a clean and effective way to do the initial foam shaping, **18-5**. After you've shaped the basic contours with the foam cutters, round off any angular edges on the

18-2

In this shallow cut, only a portion of the underlying rock is exposed. The rest of the exposed facing is primarily soil. Notice that the rock face in this case is relatively smooth and unstratified.

hilltop with sandpaper. Once you are satisfied with the basic hill and cut-face contours that you've carved in the foam blocks, glue them in place with a hot glue gun.

## Casting small rock cuts

Although there are many types of soil faces, let's look at a face cut through stratified sedimentary rock such as limestone. The exposed face in this type of rock is primarily stone with large amounts of spall running down the face of the slope. The base for the exposed rock face can be produced easily from plaster castings made with a rock mold, **18-6**. Woodland Scenics makes a mold (C1230 Rock Outcrops) that is ideal for small rock cuts, **18-7**.

To use, begin by prepping the mold with a mold release agent. While the instructions suggest wetting the mold with detergent, I've found this will occasionally produce soap bubbles and air pockets in the castings. Instead, spray some WD-40 on a paper towel and wipe a thin film of the lubricant over the mold. This step will need to be repeated before every pour. After the mold is prepped, prepare a mix of plaster of paris to the consistency of a milk shake. Pour the plaster in the mold and then tap the mold a few times to help remove any air bubbles. Once the plaster has set, remove the castings and begin another set. You'll probably need at least four or five sets of castings for one rock cut.

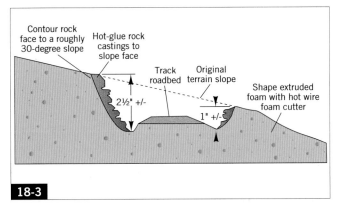

18-3

A gently rolling hill surrounds the rock cut, which has been shaped from layers of extruded foam.

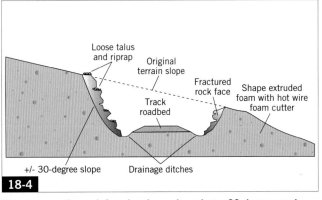

18-4

The slope on the rock face has been shaped at a 30-degree angle. Drainage ditches around the roadbed have been cut into the foam.

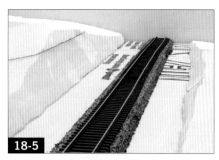

**18-5**

The basic shape of the cut has been formed out of foam on the workbench using a hot wire foam cutter. Be sure to set the rock face back far enough from the track to allow room for mounting the rock castings.

**18-6**

Rock molds and plaster of paris are ideal for creating rock castings. If you have large gaps around or behind your castings after they've been glued in place, the gaps can be filled with joint compound.

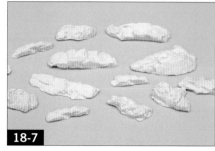

**18-7**

Rock mold castings do an excellent job of producing blockier rock faces. You will need several sets of castings to produce enough rock for a cut.

**18-8**

Spall or talus can be modeled by creating thin plaster chips and sprinkling them down the rock face.

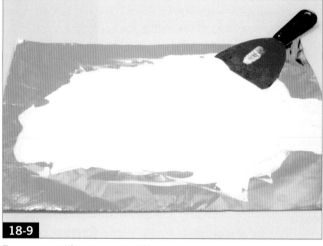

**18-9**

To create spalling, spread a thin layer of plaster of paris on aluminum foil. After it dries, crumble it into small pieces.

## Making rock strata

Excavating a rock cut produces a liberal amount of spalling, chips, and loose rock debris that accumulates in crevices or falls to the bottom of the face. To represent this spalling, which also occurs through natural erosion, you need something thin and flaky.

Plaster chips and wafers are ideal for representing this type of spalling, **18-8**. To create thin plaster chips, begin by placing a sheet of aluminum foil on your workbench. Mix up another batch of plaster of paris but make it a touch runnier than one used for rock molds. Pour the mix onto the aluminum foil, **18-9**. Use a spatula or putty knife to spread the plaster into a sheet as smooth and thin as you can make. Allow the plaster to dry completely. When it is dry, pick up the thin plaster sheet and crumble it into smaller pieces as if you were crumbling up a cracker. Scoop up the pieces and put them in a plastic bag for later use.

## Gluing the castings

At this point, you have the rock outcrops and spall necessary for modeling an exposed rock cut face. The next step is to glue the rock outcrops to the foam base using a hot glue gun, **18-10**. Alternate your castings, flipping some upside down to make it less obvious that you are using the same casting more than once. For additional variety, cut some of the castings into smaller pieces with a pair of side cutters. Cover the entire face of your foam base leaving as few gaps as possible between castings. If you find any gaps behind or between your castings that are too large, you can fill them in with joint compound.

## Adding loose chips

Next, lightly sprinkle the plaster chips over the rock face, starting at the top of the rock face, **18-11**. Start at the top of the rock face and work downward. Use a spoon to poor small quantities of chips into the gaps between your castings. When you are satisfied with the overall look of your plaster chips, fix them in place with diluted glue (three parts water and one part white glue). You can substitute matte medium for the white glue if you want the chips to have a less-glossy appearance when they are dry.

## Staining the rock

After your castings and talus have been glued in place and the glue has dried, the next step is to add a touch of color. Here, a light hand is necessary. If your final color is too light, it is a simple matter to gradually darken it. If the color is too dark, it is difficult to lighten. To tint the rock, acrylic earth-tone paints, such as very light grays or beige, are a good choice, **18-12**. To create a diluted rock stain, fill a plastic cup with water and add a splash or two of rubbing alcohol to act as a dispersal

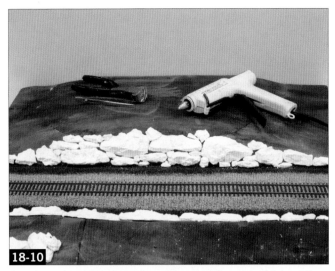

**18-10**

Glue the rock castings in random patterns on the exposed face of the cut. You can use side cutters to break the castings into smaller pieces.

**18-11**

Plaster chips have been sprinkled down the rock face to represent spall. Fix them in place with diluted white glue.

agent. Next, add a few drops of acrylic craft paint and mix thoroughly. Again, the mix should be very dilute. Pour the diluted paint into a spray bottle and test the color on a scrap piece of plastic to make sure it isn't too dark. When satisfied with your color mix, spray it liberally over your castings and let them dry, **18-13**.

## Finishing the scene

After the stained rocks dry, you can complete the scene by bringing your scenery vegetation up to the edges of the rock outcrop, **18-14**. During the winter, earth-toned vegetation is the order of the day but even in the harsh-

est months, a touch of green sprouts up here and there. Start with a base layer of beige static grass and perhaps some dried leaves. Next, bring some trees up the edge of the cut. SuperTrees armatures from Scenic Express, painted with gray primer, make good winter trees. Sprinkle some dried twigs over the top lip of the cut and scatter a few twigs down the face. Finally, examine the side of the rock face to make sure none of the foam scenery backing shows through the gaps between your castings. If there are a few holes where the foam shows through, simply cover these up with strategically placed twigs or additional riprap.

**18-12**

Earth tones such as light gray or beige make a good base for coloring a rock cut.

**18-13**

Spray very dilute mixes of acrylic earth-tone paint onto the castings to add subtle color tones.

**18-14**

Surrounding winter vegetation is brought up to and around the castings. Actual twigs are as fallen trees, and SuperTrees, painted with gray primer, represent saplings growing out of the cracks. Model dead winter ground cover with beige static grass.

19-1

CHAPTER NINETEEN   by Mike Danneman

# Ice and snow

A westbound freight enters the Cliff siding while the rest of the train snakes alongside frozen South Boulder Creek in this view on my N scale Rio Grande layout. Adding snow to your layout might not be as difficult as you think.

Winter is probably one of the least modeled times of year. The thought of heading downstairs to run some trains on a cold winter's day is surely less appealing if, when you turn the layout room lights on, all you see is icy, snow-covered scenery.

**19-2**

I glued Hydrocal plaster rock castings to the scenery base using a low-temp hot glue gun. To blend and hide the edges, I applied Sculptamold between the rock castings and horizontal seams.

**19-3**

The scenery is now colored and tinted with an inexpensive earth-colored latex paint and acrylic paints.

**19-4**

I glued riprap in slope areas and along the creek. The extremely vertical rock-work is part of the transition area along the backdrop that will help disguise the joint between the scenery and backdrop.

**19-5**

After finishing the coloring of the scenery, I masked off the track, creekbed, and fascia and then began the application of a Hydrocal snowstorm.

Many layouts have a small area of scenery covered with a dusting of snow, perhaps to represent a high mountain region. But I think many people shy away from modeling winter because it might seem difficult to permanently model snow and ice effects. Or perhaps it is the daunting thought of keeping all that white scenery clean. And just how can you model snow on the track without interfering with the operation of the trains? Modeling winter may seem like a difficult task, **19-1**.

With the right tools and materials, winter can be modeled successfully. Let's model some winter scenery and maybe you'll change your mind. Besides, when the air conditioner is humming on a hot, humid summer day, it might be very refreshing to head downstairs and run a few trains through the snow.

One of the biggest tasks I faced when modeling winter on my layout was finding the right materials, so I decided to test different commercial materials used for modeling snow. I constructed a small diorama, complete with roadbed and track, for testing the materials. This way I did not have to experiment, and possibly damage, any scenery on my layout.

## Making it snow

Through testing, I found out which materials I preferred and which ones worked better for certain applications. For example, on the larger expanses of the layout that were to be covered with snow, I liked the way simple Hydrocal plaster represented freshly fallen snow. Lightweight Hydrocal is very white, which makes it a great material for snow. The secret is in how you apply it.

Before you add any snow to your winter scene, you have to model the scenery it covers. The underlying scenery such as the landforms and rock must be constructed and colored first, **19-2** and **19-3**. Model the scene as you would see it in the winter months—without the snow cover. Some scenery materials like trees can be added later, but it is important to get the scenery as compete as possible. Decide where creeks, buildings, roads, and other scenic elements will go. I installed riprap and other rock materials along the right-of-way and ballasted and painted the track as well, **19-4**.

Once your scenery is completed to this point, you might be like me and have second thoughts about covering up all that nice finished scenery with snow. But don't stop and change your mind

**19-6**

Once the Hydrocal is applied to the desired depth and sets, remove the masking. The track, roads, creek, and other scenery elements can then be winterized.

**19-7**

Nothing ruins the realism of a snow scene more than everything being nicely covered in snow except the track. Snow effects on the roadbed have to be treated differently than the rest of the scenery but can be applied with simple ballasting techniques. In this scene, Tunnel Motor 5359 leads a coal empty into Cliff over freshly fallen snow.

on what season to model. Gathering up enough courage one evening, I just started masking all the track, highways and roads, streambeds, and the edge of the fascia and then dove in, **19-5**. I masked places where I didn't want any snow cover quite yet as well as objects on which I was going to use other snow-modeling techniques.

I misted the scenery using a spray bottle filled with "wet water" (water and a few drops of dish soap). I then grabbed an ordinary kitchen sieve and sifted dry Hydrocal over the scene. Let it snow! I wetted it again to make sure the Hydrocal was soaked. I then sifted on a little more, and it looked pretty good. I let the Hydrocal set up, and to my satisfaction, it was nice and solid. Any areas that aren't misted completely will be powdery. The secret is to make sure that all the Hydrocal gets thoroughly wet—but not so it drips and runs all over everything. To increase the depth of the snow, just repeat the steps. After you have the snow depth that you are looking for, you can pull the masking tape off the track, roads, and other areas that need additional winter effects, **19-6**.

For covering large areas, you can also use Woodland Scenics snow or other commercial products. They just have to be handled in a different manner. As I did, test these snow materials on a diorama to see if you like how they

look. Before applying any snow to your layout, complete the base scenery first as was done with the Hydrocal. Then, thoroughly spray the finished scenery with wet water and gently sift the snow over the scene. You will then need to glue the snow in place just like ground foam or similar scenery materials using a diluted matte medium or white glue solution.

## Adding snow to the track

One of my biggest concerns was finding a scenery material that I could use on my track to represent snow. I wanted the snow-covered track to be durable and have no obstructions that inhibited train operation. I wanted the track to look like a railroad with freshly fallen snow with just a pair of rails slicing through the scene, **19-7**. Testing commercial snow products helped me find what I was looking for.

I tested several materials with differing results. Woodland Scenics snow looked pretty nice, but since I model N scale, I thought that this snow material was a bit too granular. It would work very well for larger scales. I decided on using Arizona Rock & Mineral snow on the track. Arizona Rock snow is essentially white marble dust, which is the consistency of a heavy powder. If you cannot find Arizona Rock scenery materials, you might be able to locate marble dust in craft, art supply, or home improvement stores. Spread this snow

on the track as though it were ballast. I wanted it to look like the trains have been plowing the snow, **19-8**, but how deep you want to model it is up to you.

I carefully groomed the marble dust over the track using a simple, home-made wood template. I used wood for this clearance template to prevent scraping the previously painted rail sides. I cut notches into the template and added small pieces of stripwood to keep the snow out of the flangeways and keep the overall level of the marble dust lower than the rail height.

Just as you ballast your track, it pays to be extremely careful when grooming the marble dust. Once all of the marble dust was nicely groomed, I thoroughly wet it and then glued it with matte medium solution (matte medium diluted 3:1 with water and a few drops of dish soap as a wetting agent). While the marble dust was still wet, I used wooden toothpicks to clean any granules of marble dust that crept up the sides of the rails. I also carefully cleaned any errant globs of wet marble dust out of the flangeways. Removing unwanted marble dust while it is wet is important, since once it is dry, the

19-8

Operation managers have called out a plow train to take care of the heavy accumulation of snow occurring in higher elevations. Spreader AX-41 and two GP30s answer the call and are headed westbound near Cliff. Winter scenery can even add to the operations of your layout.

19-9

Ice builds up over still-flowing South Boulder Creek just below the site of former Tunnel 8. Winter effects like ice and snow on exposed rocks really add to a scene. The thin ice sheets are made using casting resin.

marble dust sets up like concrete, much like well-bonded ballast.

When the marble-dust snow on the track dried, I noticed it was slightly yellow compared to the stark white Hydrocal snow adjoining it. I don't know if the marble dust is not truly white after you wet it or if the matte medium dries with a slightly yellow cast to it. But we all know what mom told us about yellow snow! It ended up being an easy fix. I diluted some gesso, which is a pure-white medium for priming an artist's canvas, with water (about 1:1 to 1:2 will work) and applied a wash over the marble-dust roadbed, being careful to not get any on the rails. It took several coats, but soon it was as white as the surrounding scenery.

On my layout, I found that keeping track clean in a snow scene does take some extra care and patience. With deep snow almost up to the top of the rails in some locations, and small snowbanks lining the roadbed, you can't just swipe a Bright Boy down the rails. The track has to be cleaned much more methodically and slowly, and usually only one rail at a time. One slip with a dirty Bright Boy will leave a nice black streak in the snow. But if this happens, a black streak can be cleaned up by lightly scraping it off the surface of the marble-dust snow and touching up the area with diluted gesso. When cleaning the snow scene on my layout, I sympathize with those traction modelers that have all of that intricate street trackage to keep clean!

## Creating snowy special effects

Along with track, scenic elements such as trees, creeks, roads, and structures are modeled for winter using some slightly different scenery techniques. Follow along to add some snowy, icy effects to these features on your layout.

### Winterizing a creek

Once I removed the masking tape and vacuumed all the loose pieces of Hydrocal from the main snow cover, it was time to finish the creek, **19-9**. I painted the creekbed a deep bluish-black color, which I had used around previously planted rocks and boulders in the creekbed. Any rocks that were to be left underwater were painted with this same dark color. Once the paint was dry in the creekbed, I added several layers of acrylic gloss medium to represent flowing water. Add as many layers as you want to build up the water depth. Be sure to apply only thin layers of the gloss medium to avoid cracking and crazing. Once the water is dry, and you are happy with its appearance, dry-brush some white paint on spots to represent the white water of a fast-moving mountain stream. In winter, some creeks remain open while others become covered with ice and snow. Now comes the fun part, winterizing your creek!

The boulders sticking up through the water can be topped with snow after a fresh snowfall. For coating the tops of these exposed rocks, I use a thick gesso to represent the snow. This elastic material has a flat finish, is unaf-

fected by light or water, and does not yellow. It also comes in handy for any touch-up work between the Hydrocal snow and other snow scenery.

For areas of deeper snow, I use another art product, Liquitex modeling paste, which is a matte, opaque preparation of marble dust and polymer emulsion. While gesso may crack when applied too thickly, modeling paste doesn't and works well for areas needing more snow depth. Using thick gesso and modeling paste makes finishing up any needed snow effects much easier.

### Modeling a snow-covered road

To model a winter highway or road, you first have to actually model the pavement. For the highway on my layout, I cut sheet styrene to the road's dimensions and painted it the appropriate color. Depending on how much snow you plan to have on your roadway, you'll need to add road markings such as dashed or solid painted lines at this time too.

I added the snow effects to the road in small sections at a time. I poured thinly mixed Hydrocal directly onto the road surface and spread it out to the approximate depth of snow I wanted. I then used a freely rolling vehicle to make ruts in the snow. (An N scale vehicle in my case, and don't use your favorite one!) As the wet plaster set, I rolled the car back and forth, rinsing off the vehicle before the Hydrocal set. By working in small sections, I was able to keep up with the fast-setting

**19-10**

A plow has cleared one lane of the highway, and the driver of the auto behind the plow should have removed more snow from the windshield for better visibility! Winter details, such as Woodland Scenics Snowball Fight (no. 785-2183), in this scene add to the realism.

**19-11**

The roofs of the buildings in this snow scene were misted with wet water and covered with Hydrocal. I added the snow at my workbench, so I had more control of the Hydrocal plaster and its quick-setting tendencies.

**19-12**

Icicles can be made using a two-part casting resin and waxed paper. An employee toting a shovel, ready for another day's work in the snowy mountains of Colorado, walks past some eye-catching icicles.

Hydrocal. It a few areas, I let the road pavement show through realistically. For an added touch, I cleared one of the lancs with a small piece of wood (to prevent scraping the painted surface of the road) to represent the passing of a highway snowplow, **19-10**.

The snow-covered highway now had a nice rutted look, but the thinness of the Hydrocal made it somewhat fragile. To remedy this, once the Hydrocal was dry, I added some diluted matte medium with an eyedropper to strengthen the snow, just as you would when affixing any other scenery material.

## Covering structures with snow

For adding snow to the rooftops of the structures, I also used Hydrocal, **19-11**. I took the structures off the layout and separately added snow to each one. First, I misted the roof with wet water. I then sifted Hydrocal onto the roof with an ordinal kitchen sieve (preferably one not to be used in the kitchen again), until I had a nice thin, even layer. I then misted more water onto the roof until the Hydrocal was thoroughly soaked but not dripping.

While letting each layer on a roof set, I continued to apply more Hydrocal and wet water until I had a depth of snow that matched that of the surrounding scenery. On one structure with a smooth roof, the snow broke off in one piece like a Hydrocal casting, and I simply glued it back onto the roof. To strengthen the edges of the snow on the roofs, especially where the snow is thin, an application of diluted matte medium will do the trick. Other scenery items like telephone poles and autos were winterized in the same method. For any objects or areas that will get some abuse, make sure to add some diluted matte medium for strength.

## Creating ice effects

I modeled the thin ice sheets for my creek using casting resin, **19-9**. First, I placed a sheet of waxed paper on a level surface and mixed a small amount of two-part casting resin according to its instructions. I poured this resin onto the waxed paper in random small puddles and various shapes. For an added icy look, I sprinkled a liberal amount of

**19-13** A westbound freight roars through tiny Tunnel 29 east of Pinecliffe, Colo., past hundreds of trees that were flocked using a simple recipe of Hydrocal plaster and wet water.

**19-14** After a spring snowstorm, notice how beautiful the trees look flocked with snow. A heavy blanket of snow sticks to the outer branches of the trees.

powdered glass (picked up at a craft store) right onto the casting resin puddles. I then took a second piece of waxed paper and put it on top of the casting resin. Press the two sheets together very lightly, being careful not to let any ooze out the edges. Then, while the resin is still wet, pull the two sheets apart and let it cure. You will now have hundreds of differently shaped pieces of sparkling ice to install on your flowing creek. These pieces of ice can be used in many other applications in your winter scenery.

You can also make icicles in a similar fashion using casting resin and waxed paper. Mix a small amount of casting resin but, instead of spreading it out on the waxed paper in small puddles, take a stick and spread the resin out in stringy, random patterns. It helps to let the casting resin set up a bit to get the material to act stringy. Let the resin cure, and when it dries, you'll be able to pick through the pieces and find some that nicely represent icicles. Don't worry if a lot of the resin isn't usable, that's normal. You can glue the icicles to the edges of structure roofs, rocks, or any place some flowing water might freeze and create an icicle. Details like these icicles might be awfully small, but they do catch a viewer's eye in a winter scene, **19-12**.

## Flocking evergreens

One of the most eye-catching scenes of winter is a grove of evergreens all flocked with icy snow. It might seem a big challenge to reproduce this effect for a winter model railroad scene, but it isn't as hard as you might think.

On my Rio Grande Moffat Road, I model springtime in the Rockies. At higher elevations, such as my Pinecliffe, Colo., scene, springtime always means wet, heavy snowfalls. The area surrounding the tiny town of Pinecliffe is heavily forested with evergreens. My plan was to model a deep snowfall, so I wanted to model the trees to look like they had a heavy blanket of wet snow sticking to all the branches, **19-13**.

I began with fully finished evergreen trees. In my case, I built hundreds of trees from a material called bumpy chenille. Even though the trees will be covered in snow, it is important to form, texture, and color the trees as if they had no snow. You could also use finished commercial trees. I find it easier to flock the trees off the layout because you will have more control over the coverage. Flocking trees can be somewhat messy, which is another reason why I like to work on these trees in the garage or even outdoors. For handling the trees during the process, I simply stick the trees into small blocks of insulation foam.

For flocking evergreens, Hydrocal is again the best material. To begin, mist the trees with wet water using a fine atomizer spray bottle. Next, take a kitchen sieve and sift the dry Hydrocal over the wet trees. You'll notice how the dry Hydrocal builds up on the outer branches just as snow does on a wintery day.

You can add more snow to the trees by wetting the trees again and adding more sifted Hydrocal. Add plenty of wet water to the point where it appears that the Hydrocal is about to drip off the trees. This will assure that the Hydrocal flocking is thoroughly soaked so that it will properly set up, locking it on the outer branches of the tree, **19-14**. These steps can be continued until you have the depth of the snow you are looking for. Let's say you are modeling a scene with six inches of snow. Try to visualize what the trees would look like with six inches of snow flocked on them.

Once the Hydrocal is dry, you'll be amazed at how durable this flocking is, especially if the Hydrocal was completely soaked with water before it set up. If you ever spilled some wet Hydrocal onto your carpeting and then let it set up before you removed it, you'll know how sturdy it is!

Adding some shadow depth to the snow is an effect that will highlight the snow flocking on the trees. I mix a small amount of sky blue color with water and apply it with an atomizing spray bottle. Lightly mist one side of a tree with this blue tone, making sure to keep the tone very light. Then apply another light layer of Hydrocal over the top of the trees to give the blue shadow areas more depth. When planting the trees on you layout, make sure the sides of the trees with the bluish shadows face away from your light source.

20-1

Photos by the author

CHAPTER TWENTY    by Lance Mindheim

# Streams with flowing water

A simple 30-foot plate girder bridge is all it takes to hop over this small creek along the Western Maryland right-of-way. Scenes such as this are repeated several times a mile along many roads.

Massive rivers and dramatic waterfalls may make for nice calendar art, but if a modeler's goal is to capture the features most seen, then a meandering brook fills the bill. If you were to sit in the cab of locomotive as it makes its journey, you'd likely see several crossings of narrow waterways every mile, **20-1**. Incorporating some of these creeks and streams into a winter layout adds viewing interest and takes up very little room.

Before you get started with modeling a typical creek, run down to a local stream and take a few photographs, **20-2**. When looking at your prototype stream images, take note of some of the key characteristics such as the shape of the meanders, how and where sandbars form, and how the banks are undercut on the outside of the meanders, **20-3**.

**20-2**

To model a stream convincingly, photos of an actual stream are useful guides. This photos shows details such as sandbars, fallen trees, exposed rocks, and undercuts.

Look at how dead trees lean over the waterway and eventually topple in. Stumps and branches will usually trap leaves and smaller debris on the upstream side. Except in the coldest of months, moving water generally does not freeze over. Unless there has been a period of heavy rain, white water will be limited or nonexistent. Finally, note the width of your typical stream. Smaller waterways, 10 to 20 feet wide, occur in nature in greater abundance than those that are wider.

## Carving the stream

My preferred sub-base for scenery is extruded foam (the pink or blue insulation material). It is firm yet easy to carve and sand into the appropriate landforms, **20-4**. Using photos of actual streams as a guide, mark the route of your waterway with chalk or other erasable medium on the foam sub-base, **20-5**. If you are not satisfied with the outline of the stream route simply wipe it off with a wet rag and start over.

For the most part, a width of 2" to 5" is adequate for a typical stream. Make sure to include gentle meanders for interest. As the stream approaches the backdrop, curve it to one side and gradually taper the stream to a point and hide the end in a small grove of trees, **20-6**. This makes a better transition than running the stream at a 90-degree angle into the backdrop.

Once you are satisfied with the steam's route, it is time to carve the banks and streambed. Carving a depression into extruded foam is one of the easier ways to form the basis for your stream, **20-7**. When making your cut, be careful not to go too deep. Using a hot wire foam cutter, slowly remove material until you have a depth of about ¾". Leave the bottom flat for now. Refer to prototype photos for placing undercuts where the stream has eroded the banks as well as for adding slopes for sandbars on the opposite side of the meander. Once you have the basic shape, smooth everything out with coarse sandpaper. Sanding sticks are helpful in forming undercuts, **20-8**. Finally, sand a shallow (¼" deep) bowl shape in the bottom of the foam for the waterway itself. After the stream is excavated, paint the foam a neutral earth tone using acrylic paint.

## Texturing the banks

Since stream banks often erode to a vertical or very steep slope, it can be difficult to make earth scenery materials stick to the surface using traditional means. A simple and effective way around this problem is to create a stiff soil paste and simply paint it on the banks. Take a small amount of scenery earth and place it into a container. Take diluted white glue (three parts water, one part white glue, and a dash of rubbing alcohol) and slowly mix it into your soil, **20-9**. When done, simply paint your soil mix on the slopes and allow it to dry, **20-10**.

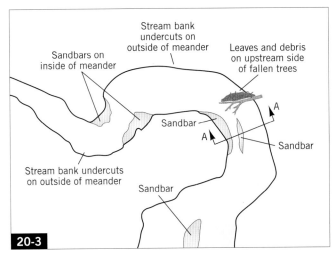

**20-3**

When planning a stream, incorporate how a stream meanders, creates undercuts, and leaves sandbars. (20-4 shows a close-up view of A-A.)

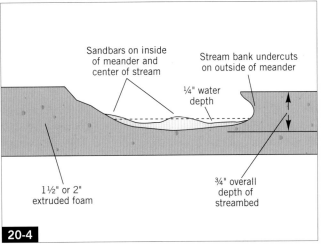

**20-4**

Carving a depression in extruded foam is easy, just be careful not to go to deep. Here, the streambed is ¾" deep.

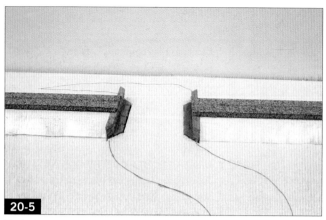

**20-5**

Mark the stream route on the foam. For most streams, a width of 2" to 5" is typical.

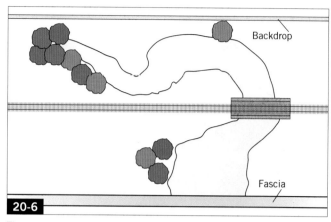

**20-6**

The stream narrows and curves to the side near the backdrop, which makes a better transition than running it perpendicular to the backdrop.

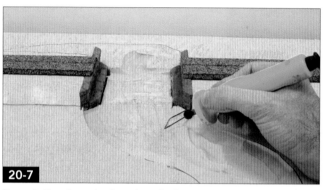

**20-7**

Excavate the channel using a hot wire foam cutter, smooth everything with coarse sandpaper, and then sand a shallow bowl for the waterway.

**20-8**

Sanding sticks are handy for forming stream undercuts, which form on the outside of meanders.

## Detailing the stream bottom

After the banks have dried, you can begin to detail the stream bottom, **20-11**. The best results are obtained by combining a detailed stream bottom with a relatively shallow water depth. First, lay down a soil mix of grays and browns. Some ballast suppliers offer soil mixes specifically designed for streambeds. Finer N and Z scale ballasts also work well. If possible, avoid larger, round boulders. One nice effect is to apply a light dusting of fine plaster chips down the center of the stream bottom. Grind small chunks of plaster until they are the size of a pinhead and lightly dust them on. Finally, sprinkle on a very light dusting of fine ground-up leaves and twigs. When dusting on this ground-up natural vegetation, keep the pieces small.

## Pouring resin

Once your stream bottom has been detailed and dried, it's time to pour the water, **20-12**. Envirotex Lite resin, available at most craft stores, works well. For the most part, this is a stable material that is easy to work with if you follow the directions. On rare occasions, however, a bad batch or old batch makes it onto the store shelves. The most obvious symptom of getting a bad batch is that resin that remains tacky and never fully cures. In order to avoid this problem, I always make a small test pour on a scrap of foam just to make sure I have a good batch.

Prior to making your pour, make sure there are no pinholes in your stream bottom and dam both ends of the stream. I've found that wax paper wrapped around a scrap of foam makes a very effective dam. After mixing the resin according to the directions, slowly pour your stream. In most cases, I make the waterway ⅛" to ¼" deep. Keep it shallow! It is not necessary or desirable to go much deeper than that. I strongly suggest not adding color to your resin mix. Let the natural colors of your streambed create the color of your waterway.

After you pour the resin, you will need to babysit it for the first hour to remove the air bubbles that rise to the surface. You can do this by exhaling on the bubbles or waving a multipurpose lighter quickly over the surface. If you chose to use the open flame of a lighter, work carefully. Although the resin is not flammable, many scenery supplies, such as trees and foam, are. Check the resin for new air bubbles every five minutes or so. It generally takes about an hour for all of the trapped air bubbles to form and rise to the surface. When you are satisfied that no more air bubbles are forming, let the resin dry overnight.

## Creating ripples

After the resin has cured, you will have fairly realistic-appearing water with a sense of depth. In order to go the extra mile, there are a few touch-up steps required. Resin has a tendency to wick up the stream banks. To repair this wicking effect, revisit the stream banks with a small brush and your muddy mixture to touch up the banks down to the water line.

**20-9**

Make a soil paste of scenery earth and diluted white glue, striving for the consistency of a very thick milk shake, and use it on steep stream banks.

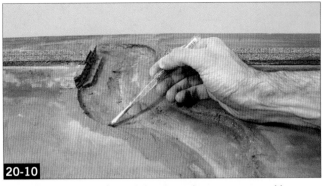

**20-10**

Paint the mix on the sides of the channel to represent muddy stream banks.

**20-11**

Detail your stream bottom using a mix of gray rail ballasts, small plaster chips, and tiny twigs.

**20-12**

The water is made of Envirotex Lite epoxy resin. For best results, keep the stream shallow and allow the colors of your streambed to color the water as well.

**20-13**

Dabbing gloss medium onto the surface of the dried Envirotex epoxy creates convincing looking ripples in the surface.

**20-14**

This overhead view of the completed stream shows vegetation flourishes around the water up to the edges of the stream and a light dusting of baking-soda snow.

The cured resin will also be unrealistically smooth. To add subtle ripples, take a watercolor brush, dip it in gloss medium, and gently dab the stream surface with vertical stabbing motions, **20-13**. If you are modeling standing or slow-moving water, which is the most common, the addition of the gloss medium completes the process of creating the water.

If you are modeling a faster moving stream, add white caps by lightly dry-brushing on white acrylic paint. If you do add white caps, be careful not to overdo it.

## Scenicking the area

Finally, bring your surrounding vegetation up to the riverbank, **20-14**. Often, vegetation will be thicker adjacent to a stream than in the surrounding areas. As a stream erodes its banks, trees will be undercut, tip, and eventually fall into the waterway. Fallen limbs tend to trap leaves, brush, and other debris on the upstream side. Most of the surrounding vegetation will be brown and gray leafless trees and shrubs. However, even in winter, there are generally still a few green weeds, evergreens, and grass patches. Small pieces of sage or azalea bushes make for realistic-looking dead limbs and fallen trees. A light dusting of baking soda adds a nice look of snow without obscuring the underlying vegetation.

21-1

CHAPTER TWENTY-ONE    by Kent Johnson

# Winter along the Timber Trail

Winter along the Cascade & Timber Trail Ry. begins with patches of ice made of clear caulk and Styrofoam snow.

When you envision winter on a model train layout, you most likely think of a layout covered in a thick blanket of artificial snow. But if you're just looking to suggest that there's a chill in the air and Christmas is coming soon, here's a few tips for adding winter scenery that do not require a total transformation of your layout. From white caulk clinging to the treetops to drifts made of craft foam, I'll share several easy ways to usher in winter weather—without making a mess and providing you with a temporary touch of wintry weather. [*Although these methods were applied to an O gauge layout (Classic Toy Trains' Cascade & Timber Trail Ry.), the same principles and materials can be used on other scale layouts, as seen on Mike Confalone's layout in Chapter 3.*]

**21-2**

A light application of caulk is effective in representing patchy, melting snow. If too much is a applied, the excess can easily be removed.

**21-3**

Pieces of ½"-thick Styrofoam turn into piles of snow with some simple tearing and compression.

**21-4**

Icicle and patches of ice can be achieved by using clear weatherstripping caulk. The easy-to-use material sets in minutes.

**21-5**

By adding some diseased trees and brown ground foam among the green, you obtain a more realistic look to an early winter scene.

**21-6**

Miniature lights add a holiday touch to buildings. This black bear will soon be heading into hibernation.

Winter arrives early in the mountains of our logging railway, so that's where I concentrated my efforts to add seasonal elements, **21-1**. The heavy snows will be arriving soon, but for now, the cold nights bring light flurries and ice that partially melt throughout the day. This freeze-and-thaw cycle results in a mix of exposed ground and patches of snow.

## Letting it snow

The first hint of snow starts at the treetops. I used a putty knife to lightly frost the pine limbs with DAP's Kwik Seal kitchen and bath adhesive caulk (similar white adhesive caulk can be used). A modest application is effective and is easier to brush off if you want to remove it from the trees later, **21-2**.

Even by day, tall trees keep snow chilled in the shade. To make piles of snow, I broke irregular, 1" pieces from a ½ x 12 x 36-inch sheet of craft Styrofoam, **21-3**. I then molded and compressed the Styrofoam pieces into shape with my finger and placed them around trees, rocks, and structures. For deeper piles, several pieces can be bonded together with white glue. The Styrofoam sheets (not insulation or bead) can be found online as well as at Jo-Ann Fabric, Michaels, and other craft stores. You can use Woodland Scenics no. ST1432 foam nails to temporarily hold the snow piles to a foam scenery base.

## Making ice

In the shadows of the cliffs and the tunnel, melting snow turns to ice. To make

some ice, I used Zip-A-Way removable sealant. I flattened beads of the clear weatherstripping caulk on wax paper to produce frozen puddles, which I placed on the track and other icy spots. I applied small strings of the material to the tunnel portal as icicles, **21-4**. The easy-to-remove icicles can also be added to building roofs and overhangs.

## Adding details

Since winter has not fully arrived, much of the forest floor is still visible. And at this time of year, scenery colors are muted. For forest foliage, brown is in, **21-5**. I covered patches of ground with Scenic Express no. EX830B brown turf to represent decaying brush and leaves. I also planted a few diseased trees, adding spots of brown among the green pines.

For some festive, holiday touches, you can add a string of miniature lights or LEDs to a house or even to a small evergreen tree during Christmastime. I added a set of miniature lights

(Department 56 no. 53187) to one of the logging camp shacks, **21-6**. When using LEDs, 3mm lights work best on O and HO layouts while 1.8mm can be used for N scale.

You can also have figures on your layout enjoy a fire by roasting chestnuts, singing carols, or just warming up. I sunk a battery-powered tealight candle (Smart Candle no. SC3684A-C6) into the scenery base and covered the flame-shaped bulb with firewood. You can do the same on an HO layout or use one of the LED fire kits that are available (Evan Designs or GRS Micro Liting).

When the cool weather hits, make sure your figures and vehicles are ready for the weather. For operation in snow, add trucks with tire chains and plows, snowmobiles, and work vehicles with tracks and skids. Use figures dressed for the cool weather and engaged in winter activities. And don't forget the wildlife. Remove any critters that migrate or hibernate during the winter months.

22-1

Photos by the author

CHAPTER TWENTY-TWO    by Mike Danneman

# Winter backdrop tips

Three Union Pacific SD70Ms pull a stack train through a snowy canyon. In this scene, I used scenery materials at the interface of the scenery and backdrop to disguise the transition. Don't be afraid to use scenery materials on your backdrop or backdrop paints on your scenery to accomplish this.

When you think of winter, you naturally think of snow. To model winter on your layout, you may not necessarily have to add snow as scenery, but you should show some on your backdrop, **22-1**. And, as in nature, snow can provide a dramatic background scene, especially when combined with mountains, **22-2**.

Surprisingly, the biggest tip I can give for a winter backdrop is to paint a summer one first. Well, that's not entirely true. You wouldn't want to put snow on top of your nice green deciduous trees. What I mean is that you have to first paint the winter scenery on the backdrop as it would appear without any snow on it.

**22-2**

This eastbound freight cruises through Grizzly, Mont., on the east slope of Marias Pass. The spectacular mountain range is partially obscured by snowy clouds, which would make for a less-common backdrop scene.

**22-3**

Rock formations break up the evergreens on the distant mountains, and the trees have taken on a bluish cast. Carefully applying soupy blobs of Hydrocal is a great way to model the melting snow on the rooftops.

**22-4**

The sun has begun to melt some of the snow on the exposed southern flanks of the mountains. It is easy to see where the snow naturally accumulates and easy to replicate theses depths on a backdrop.

**22-5**

Using titanium white acrylic paint, I stippled the tree-covered areas to represent trees covered with snow flocking. On exposed rocks, I added some upper edging with white paint to simulate freshly fallen snow.

Picture what a gloomy winter day looks like without snow on the ground: yellow or dead grass, bare trees, and patches of earth. You have to visualize winter scenery and your backdrop this way. Then, after you have painted all the backdrop scenery, you can let it snow. When I painted the backdrop for my Pinecliffe, Colo., scene on my N scale Rio Grande Moffat Road, I painted the scenery as it might appear during a much warmer time of year. In the mountains above the small town, I broke up masses of evergreens with scattered rock faces, **22-3**.

Then add snow on what appears to be as a finished backdrop. A soft covering of snow seems to brighten up everything on a stark, winter day. Add snow to the backdrop where it would naturally gather, leaving places too steep or under cover without snow, **22-4**. Use titanium white to paint the snow and, by adding small amounts of sky-blue color, you can produce a sense of coolness that will enhance the snow effects. On my layout, I stippled titanium white paint over the tree-covered mountains. The distant trees were made to look as if they were flocked with fresh snow, **22-5**. To do so, stipple the white paint as though the snow was sticking to the outer branches of the trees. Edge the rocks with snow to define their shapes.

When painting, also consider the angle of light on the scenery from your layout's lighting, so shadows are behind the subjects. Sometimes, these blue shadow effects are most effective when they are kept subtle.

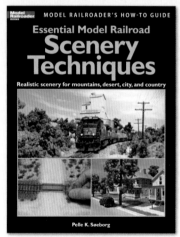
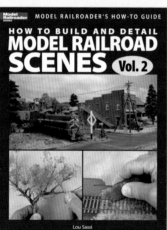
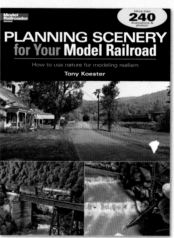
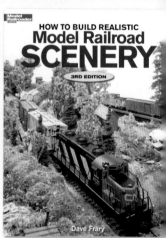